KNOW YOUR SPIRITUAL RIGHTS

END-TIMES WEAPONRY FOR THE
WARRIOR IN CHRIST

BATTLE MANUALS FOR FREEDOM
BOOK 4

A. LE ROY

UNPARAGONED

Copyright © 2024-2025 by A. Le Roy/ Abdiel LeRoy

✽ Formatted with Vellum

BATTLE MANUALS FOR FREEDOM
GENI.US/RIGHTS

Book 1: *Know Your Medical Rights*
Book 2: *Know Your Lawful Rights*
Book 3: *Know Your Financial Rights*
Book 4: *Know Your Spiritual Rights*

CONTENTS

Introduction	ix
"WHAT THE RIGHTEOUS DECREE, THE HOLY ONE CARRIES OUT."	1
Righteousness by Faith Alone	2
"What the Righteous Decree, the Holy One Carries Out."	4
COVID: THE SATANIC PLAYBOOK WRIT LARGE	6
Satan, the god of Counterfeits and Pale Imitations	8
'COVID' and the Seed War	11
FREEMASONS AND PHARMAKEIA	14
The Shylock Equation	16
Secret Societies	18
As Below, so Above?	20
The Cult of Molech	22
Harvesting the Living to Prop up the Dead	23
The Ninth Circle and 'King' Charles	25
"IT'S THE JEWS!"?	30
Jews and Freemasonry	33
A Potted History of the Seed War	36
The Talmud and Other Satanic Texts	40
Jews and Genocide	44
In Summation	51
TRAITOR TRUMP	52
The Magic Bullet of Butler	55
Your Trump Quiz	58
THE DECEPTION-INDUSTRIAL COMPLEX	64
The White-Tile Team	66

THE CHRISTIAN'S AUTHORITY IN
SPIRITUAL WARFARE 70
Binding and Loosing 72
Speaking Truth *to* Power, Not Just *About*
Power 73
Prayer Gets Results 85

PROPHETIC FULFILMENTS AHEAD 88
When We Are Judges 94
Dreams and Visions 97

INTERCESSORY DECREES

INTERCESSORY DECREE 1 109
Protecting Children, Unmasking and Demolishing the Synagogue of Satan
INTERCESSORY DECREE 2 113
On Banking, Censorship, and Surveillance
INTERCESSORY DECREE 3 116
On War
INTERCESSORY DECREE 4 119
Completion of Deliverance

Conclusion 125

FURTHER EXPLORATION

PART I
WAGING SPIRITUAL WAR

LOVE MY ENEMIES? YOU GOTTA BE
KIDDING! 135
CHRISTIANS SHOULD BE CURSING COPS 138
The Exercise of Both Logical and Spiritual Authority When Tyrants Rule
A COVID AMNESTY IS EVIL
AND UNGODLY 143
WHEN A TYRANT BEGS YOU FOR MERCY 147
YE SHALL DESTROY THE FREEMASONS 150
HOW TO TRIGGER AN ATHEIST 158

PART II
INSIGHTS FOR CHRISTIANS

NO, WE DON'T NEED 'UNITY' — 167
On the Path of Individuality

REBUKING THE CROWBAR BIBLE! — 172

DIGITAL ID — A LIVING DEATH, AND TOTAL ANNIHILATION OF SELF — 175

THERE'S NOTHING TO FEAR IN STARMER'S DIGITAL ID THREAT — 180

A CHRISTIAN CONTEMPLATES HIS EXECUTION (PROSE VERSION) — 183
When Faced With "Comply or Die"

A CHRISTIAN CONTEMPLATES HIS EXECUTION (POEM VERSION) — 186
When Faced With "Comply or Die"

SNAPSHOTS OF THE END-TIMES SHITSHOW — 189
A Portrait of Tyranny in Quotes

PART III
EXPOSING CRISIS ACTORS AND PSYCHOLOGICAL OPERATIONS

KAYLA AND THE SECRET-SERVICE CRISIS ACTORS — 205

BETRAYED BY A SANDY-HOOK CRISIS ACTOR — 208
David Cole Wheeler Sold Out His Country, Shakespeare, and All of Us

TRUMP WAS STRAIGHT MAN TO BIDEN'S CLOWN — 214
on the Biden-Trump Comedy Duo Masquerading as a Presidential Debate, June 27, 2024

TRUMP IS ANOTHER RICHARD III (AND BRANDON BIGGS IS A FRAUD) — 217

THE MAGIC BULLET OF BUTLER — 222
on Trump's Miraculous Recovery From a Purported Assassination Attempt in Butler, Pennsylvania

IN-AUGUR-ATION — 224
On Today's Installation of Trump

REST IN PURGATORY, CHARLIE KIRK — 227
On the Supposed Assassination of Media Personality, Charlie Kirk

THE LADY DOTH PROTEST TOO MUCH,
METHINKS 230
On the Histrionics of Erika Kirk, Widow to Charlatan Charlie

JEZEBERIKA 232
on the memorial for Charlie Kirk (at State Farm Stadium in Glendale, AZ, Sept. 21, 2025), and Erika Kirk's role in it

PART IV
SHORT FICTION

THE PARABLE OF THE FROGS 237
THE AWAKENING 240
KLAUS AND THE DEVIL 247

From the Author 259
Battle Manuals for Freedom 261

BOOKS BY A. LEROY (ABDIEL LEROY)

NON-FICTION 265
POETRY COLLECTIONS 271
EPIC POETRY 275
(Fiction in Verse)
FICTION 277

Notes 281

INTRODUCTION

In peace there's nothing so becomes a man
As modest stillness and humility,
But when the blast of war blows in our ears,
Then imitate the action of the tiger;
Stiffen the sinews, summon up the blood,
Disguise fair nature with hard-favor'd rage
Then lend the eye a terrible aspect.

— HENRY V, III.I.

We are in a fight to the death. Our enemy was a murderer from the beginning, and not content with merely taking souls, he must kill and torture bodies too, such is his hatred of those who are made in the image of the Most High and against true Christians in particular. Yet we are called and equipped to wield devastating spiritual violence against him and his brood. If you have no stomach for the fight, then this book is not for you.

This battle manual may challenge your perceptions, even if you are steeped in knowledge of Scripture because, as I will show, notions of loving one's enemies or blessing those who persecute you do not apply in the battles ahead. I will also banish ungodly pretensions about extending facile forgiveness, let alone 'amnesty', to the psychopaths now pursuing their triple-'e' agendas of extortion, enslavement, and extermination, followed by a fourth 'e', to exculpate themselves of their crimes.

What is needed here is some good Old-Testament Justice, such as the mass slaughter of false prophets orchestrated by Elijah on Mount Carmel (*1 Kings* 18), or Jehu ordering his men to surround a temple of Baal priests and butcher every one (*2 Kings* 10:18-27), or Queen Esther contriving the execution of a murderous official on the gallows he had built to hang an innocent man (*Esther* 7). Then there is the ultimate precedent of Moses mass slaughtering Pharaoh and his million-man army in the Red Sea (*Exodus* 14).

This book extends my analysis from *Battle Manuals for Freedom,* a three-book series I began in 2022 with *Know Your Medical Rights* (originally titled *The COVID Protocols: Upholding Your Rights in Authoritarian Times*). This was my response to the worldwide medical tyranny that began in 2020 under the banner of 'COVID'. Then, realizing that medicine was but one weapon among many targeting us, I added two more constitutional bibles, *Know Your Lawful Rights* and *Know Your Financial Rights.*

Job done, or so I thought, but the need for a fourth battle manual became apparent for we who exercise our spiritual authority in Jesus Christ to "overcome all the power of the enemy" (*Luke* 10:19), not just the logical authority we all have over Government.

Let me explain. Throughout the series, I quoted several times from the documentary film *Strawman* that, "Government is a creation of Man, and a creation of Man can never be above Man." That is our *logical* authority, as Living Men and Living Women, over everything that Government is and everything that Government creates. I also called on each of us to be a CONSTITUTIONAL EXTREMIST.

But some readers were not willing to go with me when I invoked the infinitely more powerful spiritual authority in Jesus. (*Luke* 10:19). Some even took offence, none more so than Veronica: of the Chapman family, author of *Freedom… Is More Than Just a Seven-Letter Word*. In August 2024, shortly after I published the second book, *Know Your Lawful Rights*, she sent me a torrent of angry emails telling me she did try to read it "but I'm really sorry, Abdiel. There's far and away too much utter USELESS and IRRELEVANT God/Jesus/Biblical CRAP in it… for me. If you were to remove all of that, it could be a very good book. But it would only be about 1/4 of the size" (emphases hers).

She went on to tell me she's an atheist, and it became obvious, in reading her diabolical diatribe, that atheism is her religion. The thing is, it takes an awful lot of faith to be an atheist and, in Veronica's case, a deep-seated and irrational hatred of Christians. Generally, I have far more respect for agnostics who at least have the humility to admit they don't know.

I also remind atheists that the medical butchery we are witnessing has deep religious motivation rooted in secret oaths and blood sacrifice. If you think to counter that only with the authority of logic and fail to wield *spiritual* authority—even the authority by which Jesus saw Satan fall like lightning from Heaven (*Luke* 10:18)—then you will be easy prey in the coming attacks.

Also, without the Mind of Christ (*1 Corinthians* 2:16), you will be more susceptible to deception, and without the context of Biblical prophecy, so ill-prepared for coming events that the shock could literally kill you (*Luke* 21:26). That is a very bad time to be an atheist and suddenly realize it's time to rethink your position.

So I make no attempt to accommodate the Veronicas of this world here, nor to tiptoe around their triggers. Rather, with an audience of Christians in mind, my entire focus will be on spiritual battle and the spiritual weapons at our disposal.

Another atheist response is to duck and hide from discussing the spiritual truths in play. In April 2025, I appeared for the second time on British podcaster Richard Vobes' show on YouTube. We were scheduled to talk for two hours on the subject of *Prayer to Overthrow Empire* but he cut the interview short at one hour and twenty minutes and then screened only 40 minutes of that, cutting out the most hard-hitting material.

That disappointing experience was the catalyst for this

book. Frustrated that important and possibly life-saving information was being withheld from the airwaves, I decided to put it in writing and hold nothing back.

Finally, a note about the names we use for the Most High, the Almighty, Yahweh, and so on, and for Jesus, Christ, Jesus Christ, Yeshua, the Son of Man, etc. Some purported Christians are getting way too hung up on this, some even asserting that prayers are ineffective if not addressed to their favoured title. What nonsense!

"What's in a name? That which we call a rose
By any other name would smell as sweet.
So Romeo would, were he not Romeo called,
Retain that dear perfection which he owns
Without that title."

— SHAKESPEARE, *ROMEO AND JULIET*, II.II

So *Jesus* would, were he not Jesus called, retain that dear perfection which *he* owns. He knows we are addressing him in our prayers, all Heaven and Hell know it. Nor is it godly to nitpick how you close your prayers, whether with "So be it," "Allelujah," or "Amen," etc. The Kingdom of Heaven does not concern itself with such trivialities, so for Heaven's sake, let them go, and get on with the battle to which we are called. Brothers and Sisters, we are at war, whether you like it or not, so let me be your armourer and prepare you for the fight.

Abdiel LeRoy

"WHAT THE RIGHTEOUS DECREE, THE HOLY ONE CARRIES OUT."

"I was brought up by my mother on the Bible, and she told me something that I've never forgotten. She said the stories in the Bible are stories about the conflict between the kings who have power and the prophets who preach righteousness, and she taught me to support the prophets and not the kings."

— TONY BENN, FORMER BRITISH
PARLIAMENTARIAN, 2006

We who are in Christ have barely begun to exercise our authority in prayer, but these times call on us to reclaim it. Here are some key Scriptures…

"Another angel, who had a golden censer, came and stood at the altar. He was given much incense to offer, with the prayers of all the saints, on the golden altar before the throne."

— REVELATION 8:3

Thus, our prayers are pleasing to the Most High. Also,...

"The prayers of a righteous man are powerful and effective."

— JAMES 5:16

Righteousness by Faith Alone

Now, if the qualification to be powerful in prayer is righteousness, how can any of us know that we *are* righteous? This is addressed by the apostle Paul...

"Abram believed God, and it was credited to him as righteousness."

— ROMANS 4:3

Thus, righteousness is not obtained by living a 'good' life or doing the 'right' things but is a gift conferred through faith in Christ alone. The Bible likens this righteousness to a garment...

"May your priests be clothed with righteousness; may your saints sing for joy."

— PSALM 132:9

Let us rejoice in this Truth with John Bunyan who writes, in *Grace Abounding to the Chief of Sinners* (1666),...

"But one day, as I was passing in the field, and that too with some dashes of conscience, fearing lest all was not right, suddenly this sentence fell upon my soul, Thy righteousness is in Heaven; and methought withal, I saw, with the eyes of my soul, Jesus Christ at God's right hand; there, I say, is my righteousness; so that wherever I was, or whatever I was a-doing, God could not say of me, he lacks my righteousness, for that was just before him. I also saw, moreover, that it was not my good frame of heart that made my righteousness better, nor yet my bad frame of heart that made my righteousness worse; for my righteousness was Jesus Christ himself, the same yesterday, and today, and for ever."

This is also the "mere passive righteousness" Martin Luther describes in his *Commentary on the Book of Galatians* (1531)...

"Why, do we then nothing? Do we work nothing for the obtaining of this righteousness? I answer: Nothing at all. For the nature of this righteousness is, to do nothing, to hear nothing, to know nothing whatsoever of the law or of works, but to know and to believe this only, that Christ is gone to the Father and is not now seen: that he sitteth in heaven at the right hand of his Father, not as judge, but made unto us of God, wisdom, righteousness, holiness and redemption: briefly, that he is our high-priest interceding for us, and reigning over us and in us by grace. Here, no sin is perceived, no terror or remorse of conscience is felt; for in this heavenly righteousness sin can have no place; for there is no law, and where no law is, there can be no transgression (Romans iv. 15)."

Therefore, "let us approach the throne of Grace with confidence" (*Hebrews* 4:16), where Grace means, the unmerited favour of God.

"What the Righteous Decree, the Holy One Carries Out."

An early adopter of that confidence was Moses in his struggle with Pharaoh. The pattern he follows in most of *Exodus* is to receive instructions from the Most High, after which he "did according to the word of the Lord," but as Moses grows in confidence, he can improvise in his dealings with Pharaoh whereupon "the Lord did according to the word of Moses" (*Exodus* 8:19).

So, as Dave Mason puts it in his wonderful novel, *The Lamp of Darkness*, set in the time of Elijah, "What the righteous decree, the Holy One carries out."

This changes our entire demeanour in prayer. We are not pleading or begging before the throne of the Most High but decreeing. This kind of intercession is *not*, therefore, *The General Confession*, that horrid text I dutifully recited every Sunday when a choirboy in England. I quote it now not to honour it but to mock it...

> "Almighty and most merciful Father, we have erred and strayed from thy ways like lost sheep. We have followed too much the devices and desires of our own hearts. We have offended against thy holy laws. We have left undone those things which we ought to have done; and we have done those things we ought not to have done; and there is nothing good in us. O Lord, have mercy upon us, miserable offenders."

I deconstruct this blasphemous abomination in my book, *A Better Eden*, but suffice to say for now that a son or daughter of the Most High, as Paul reminds us, is a 'slave to righteousness' (*Romans* 6:18), and no slave to righteousness has any business calling himself a 'miserable offender'!

COVID: THE SATANIC PLAYBOOK WRIT LARGE

I still remember what they'll never let themselves see:
Rez school babies crying all night, saying, "Billy, I'm
    hungry, please feed me!"
So Georgie and me we hunted for food, raiding the
    orchards at midnight,
Then I froze! I saw figures and a strange light, priests
    bending over a hole.
"Georgie, who are they?"
"Shh!" he said, "They're burying another one! Be quiet or
    we'll be dead too!"

— WILLIAM COMBES, MURDERED ON ORDERS OF 'KING' CHARLES IN FEBRUARY 2011, SOLE REMAINING EYEWITNESS TO THE ABDUCTION OF 10 NATIVE CHILDREN BY QUEEN ELIZABETH IN KAMLOOPS, CANADA, OCT. 10, 1964.

Satanic agendas have advanced at alarming speed in recent years, especially during the 'COVID' era, prompting us to cry out for Jesus' promised return. Feeling overwhelmed at times by the scale of deception and destruction now at large, we may even echo the Psalmist's lament, "my enemies are too strong for me" (*Psalm* 18:17).

We may also be tempted to watch the unfolding horrors as passive observers, telling ourselves it is futile to intervene because the end-times are coming, and only Jesus can solve this coming disaster.

Well, yes and no. It's true that every knee shall bow to Jesus (*Philippians* 2:10), that he will take vengeance on our foes with unmatched fury, that those who have loved him shall be vindicated (*Revelation* 3:9), while those who have hated him by hating us shall be put to everlasting shame. Even so, that is no reason to sit back in the meantime. Keep things simple, I say, and the simple command we have received is, "Resist the devil, and he will flee from you" (*James* 4:7).

I also infer that the reason Jesus hasn't swept in yet with the heavenly host is because the Kingdom of Heaven is within each of us, and we are already empowered to overcome all the power of the enemy. In vision, I have seen a great multitude of angels clamouring to be released to rid the Earth of its destroyers, but Jesus their captain has his hand raised. "Not yet brothers. Let my sons and daughters show their mettle first."

This is like a scene in *The Lion, the Witch and the Wardrobe* where Peter is in a fight to the death with the wolf, Maugrim. Aslan, the representation of Christ, could intervene and slay Maugrim at any time, but he refrains from doing so because he knows the boy can prevail and wants him to earn his spurs. Meanwhile, Aslan prevents a second wolf from joining Maugrim against Peter. Similarly, the Almighty defines the parameters of battle for each of us, meaning he will put us in contests that challenge us and stretch us without overwhelming us. Similarly, when Satan afflicts Job, he has to get permission from the Most High to do so, and even after he has obtained that permission, his scope of action is curtailed (*Job* 1:6-12).

Satan, the god of Counterfeits and Pale Imitations

With that in mind, let us review the enemy's playbook so that we are fully prepared to thwart his plans and defeat his offspring. If you are a Bible believer, you probably regard Satan as an angel who rebelled against the Most High and fell like lightning from Heaven (*Luke* 10:18), or perhaps you regard him more as a representation of murderous impulse, such as a dragon. In either case, the Bible serves as our battle manual to defeat him. Let us begin with Satan's origin story, as described by Isaiah…

> *"How art thou fallen from Heaven,*
> *O Lucifer, son of the dawn,*
> *You have been cast down to the Earth,*
> *You who once laid low the nations.*

"You said in your heart,
'I will ascend to Heaven,
I will raise my throne...
I will make myself like the Most High.' "

— ISAIAH 14:12-14

Thus, Lucifer, the false-light persona of Satan, will jealously imitate the Most High, but of course he can never attain to him. That is why I call him 'god of counterfeits and pale imitations'. We see this hubris in his servants too. Playing God, they want to control the weather, re-engineer genetic code, attain omniscience through surveillance, and even define what righteousness is and impose it on everyone else. They write legislation that they falsely call 'law', print currency that they falsely call 'money', issue so-called 'mandates' that they expect us to obey, and then issue so-called 'exemptions' to those mandates with a counterfeit mercy. I dare say they will follow a similar path to complete the Mark of the Beast, itself a counterfeit of the Holy Spirit's seal on those who are in Christ (*Ephesians* 1:13).

Meanwhile, they operate under a Satanic creed of 'Do what thou wilt', a counterfeit of our Christian freedom from external commandments. For a true Christian, all is distilled into loving others as we love ourselves (*Matthew* 22:39) and its derivation in Common Law to do no harm, and this is possible because we are new creations (2 *Corinthians* 5:17); we have the Law in our hearts (*Psalm* 37:31, 40:8; *Ezekiel* 36:26; *Hebrews* 10:16); our minds are set on what the Spirit desires (*Romans* 8:5); and we need no tablets of stone to guide us (*2 Corinthians* 3:3).

The Satanist's heart, on the other hand, is *made* of stone and devoted to doing harm, and the idea of loving others as itself is anathema. Nothing is freely given but demands payment be exacted, in which transaction it gives as little as possible and exacts as much as it can get away with. Its mechanism is all equation and calculation, and its contracts are one-sided impositions binding only on its unwitting victims.

But perhaps the crowning blasphemy of Satan's spawn is to play God with immortality. This is the motive of transhumanism, the idea that you can upload your consciousness into a chip and then insert that chip into a machine or cyborg or 'skin' and live forever.

That is Hell on Earth. If you or I were buried alive—Heaven forbid—we could at least die so that our souls may be released, but those who upload their consciousness into a chip bury themselves alive in silicon for eternity, and that silicon could easily be tossed into a cardboard box or landfill instead. Or, if they have uploaded their consciousness to the 'cloud', they will be trapped forever in a computer simulation from which there is no escape. This may be why *Revelation* warns, "In those days, men will long for death and not find it" (9:6).

I wouldn't mind so much if they just wanted to experiment on themselves, but it seems they want to inflict their insanity on everyone else, not by Informed Consent but by ignorant consent or falsely inferred consent or no consent at all.

'COVID' and the Seed War

Now, having learned of Satan's original rebellion, let us proceed to his first encounter with Man. After the serpent's deception that mortalized our ancestors and got them exiled from the Garden of Eden, the Almighty declares a war that is still raging to this day. "I will put enmity between thee and the woman, and between thy seed and her seed" (*Genesis* 3:15).

Satan's next move in this 'Seed War' was to adulterate Mankind's genetic code when 200 rebellious angels raped daughters of men and produced monsters and giants. This is mentioned in *Genesis* 6:4 and detailed in *First Enoch*, a book once regarded as apocryphal and kept from us, but now proving pivotal.

Those angels were imprisoned, and their Nephilim offspring wiped out by the Flood, but that was not the last attack on our genetic integrity. The COVID shots were another incursion so that, as Christian researcher and broadcaster Dustin Nemos infers, the purpose of 'Operation Warp Speed' was to warp the seed.

The COVID operation also demonstrated several more strategies Satan deploys...

   1. Jesus told us that Satan was a murderer from the beginning (*John* 8:44). Hence the

murderous protocols adopted in hospitals and nursing homes to lethally sedate the living, followed by the deadly poisons called 'vaccines'.

2. In the same verse, Jesus calls Satan the 'Father of Lies'. Hence all the propaganda and gaslighting that assailed us about so-called 'viruses' and so-called 'pandemics', and instructed us to be afraid.

3. Satan, being Prince of the Air (*Ephesians* 2:2), is also prince of the airwaves, including media and social media.

4. Satan is Accuser of the Righteous (*Revelation* 12:10). Hence the bans, shadow-bans, censorship, vilification, and demonetization of truth-tellers, whistleblowers, prophets, and investigative journalists who even questioned the medical priesthood.

5. Satan is a strainer of gnats. Jesus coined this metaphor when denouncing the Pharisees who "strain out a gnat but swallow a camel" (*Matthew* 23:24). Thus, our enemies want to imprison us or worse just for hurting someone's feelings on social media while they perpetrate genocide.

6. Satan masquerades as an angel of light, which is the character of Lucifer, and his servants masquerade as servants of righteousness (*2 Corinthians* 11:14-15). Hence all the virtue-signalling that varnishes their legislation and lies.

FREEMASONS AND PHARMAKEIA

IF Hist'ry be no ancient Fable,
Free Masons came from Tower of Babel.
When first that Fabrick was begun,
The Greatest underneath the Sun,
All Nations thither did repair
To build this Castle in the Air.
Some Thousand Hands were well employ'd
To finish what was ne'er enjoy'd.

— THE FREEMASONS: AN HUDIBRASTICK
POEM, THE DAILY POST OF LONDON,
FEB. 15, 1723

The so-called medical profession is a purveyor of great violence, you don't need me to tell you that, but the attack against Mankind unleashed under the banner of 'COVID-19'—or rather, Certificate of Vaccine

Identification AI—showed not just a willingness to do harm for profit but sadistic pleasure in doing so. It was as if the medical leadership were a priesthood demanding human sacrifice to serve infernal deities, as if doctors, nurses, hospitals, administrators, and so-called health ministers were competing to see who could add the most corpses to the pile of medical waste, or striving to meet kill quotas.

Which brings me to the 'Black Crow Award', which I first heard about from Dr. Burt Berkson. "At many medical schools, in many university hospitals," he told Dr. Jonathan Landsman in an interview, "they give an award every month to the doctor who has the most deaths on his service, and they have a party, and it's called a 'Black Crow Award'." That's what COVID was, a Black-Crow contest on a worldwide scale!

Therefore, solving the COVID crimes is not so much about follow-the-money, though Big Pharma profits immensely as governments funnel tax revenues into purchasing its poisons, but about follow-the-bodies. If it were just about follow-the-money, why would airlines inject their pilots, who represent costly investment in human capital, and jeopardize flight safety? Or why would medical-insurance companies incentivise practitioners to inject their customers, knowing this would cause their payouts to balloon?

The Shylock Equation

I call this the 'Shylock equation'. You may be familiar with the story from Shakespeare's play, *The Merchant of Venice*. Antonio is a merchant who, finding himself in a financial pinch until his ships come in, asks to borrow 3,000 ducats from Shylock to be repaid in three months. Shylock suggests,...

> *Go with me to a notary, seal me there*
> *Your single bond; and in a merry sport,*
> *If you repay me not on such a day,*
> *In such a place, such sum or sums as are*
> *Expressed in the condition, let the forfeit*
> *Be nominated for an equal pound*
> *Of your fair flesh, to be cut off and taken*
> *In what part of your body pleaseth me.*

"... in a merry sport," Shylock suggests, but we learn that he is deadly serious when Antonio defaults on the loan and Shylock, who bears him an "ancient grudge," demands his pound of flesh. When their case comes to court, Shylock is deaf to the many pleas that he show mercy to the merchant.

And this is where the Shylock equation comes in, for even when he is offered three times the sum of the original loan if he will spare Antonio, such is his loathing that he refuses, insisting on the "weight of carrion flesh." As I said, follow the bodies, not the money, especially when those who are even now sharpening their knives against us may print all the dollars they want. No, Brothers and Sisters, their coveted currency is blood.

Even so, mere population culling will not satisfy them, for they must also delight in the torture their propaganda, protocols, and products cause. First, there was the psychological torture as media mouthpieces whipped up fear, panic, and gloom during COVID; emotional torture as governments imposed isolation and kept families from elderly loved ones who were forced to die alone; and financial torture as small businesses were driven to collapse and troublesome independent journalists were demonetized.

Along with all of that came physical torture as hospitals imposed tests on every patient for a purported virus, no matter what condition or injury brought them there, generated false-positive results, and on that pretext pumped them with sedatives designed to cause respiratory failure and shut down kidney function, followed by the coup de grace of ventilators that tore the patients' lungs to shreds.

Then, from December 2020, these murderous protocols were joined by mass injection of deadly gene-altering serums into the fearful and compliant. These caused incalculable harm as they were designed to do, including autoimmune disease, for when the body's own cells are programmed to produce something harmful, such as a 'spike protein', the immune system will attack the cells that produced it.

Devilishly clever. Beyond notching up spectacular death counts, the destroyers get to enjoy their victims' suffering as they are torn apart from the inside out. When you or I see someone go into seizure after a shot, we recoil in horror, but our enemies derive sadistic satisfaction from the spectacle.

In all this, Bible prophecy is playing out. You probably don't need me to tell you that either. "By thy sorceries were all nations deceived" is the *King James Version* translation of *Revelation* 18:23. The *New International Version* has, "By your magic spell, all the nations were led astray."

In the original Greek, the word used for 'sorceries' or 'magic spell' is 'φαρμακεια', 'pharmakeia'. As explained in the Non Toxic Home blog, the term can also mean 'potion', 'poison', 'medicine', 'drug', or 'spell'.

Secret Societies

So who's behind all this? I'm going to make some obvious observations about the COVID era and draw some more than plausible inferences…

1. COVID was a marvel of coordination between nations: enacting the same tyrannical policies at the same time, writing the same vicious legislation, and pushing the same poisons.

Inference: We are not privy to the communications that facilitate this ongoing bloodbath, meaning the governments coordinate in secret—that is to say, conspire

—and secret communications require a secret network, a secret organization, a secret society.

2. Public oaths are routinely desecrated. For example, the *Hippocratic Oath* requires practitioners to do no harm, to "administer no deadly medicine," and to uphold medical confidentiality. On all three counts, they do the exact opposite. We also see police trampling their oaths, such as the *Constable's Oath* in Britain which swears to uphold "fundamental human rights." Meanwhile, politicians, bureaucrats, and judges routinely flout their oaths of office and to constitutions.

Inference: The public oath is a mere lip-service oath. Remember that Satan's servants masquerade as servants of righteousness. They pretend to serve a virtue-signalling public oath while their true loyalty is to a secret oath sworn to a secret society. Jesus had a lot to say about such hypocrisy, especially in his tirade against the Pharisees, those "whitewashed tombs, beautiful on the outside but within full of dead men's bones and everything unclean" (*Matthew* 23:27).

Jesus also confirmed that dual oath swearers are done for at the Judgment. Though they plead good works to him, he says, "Away from me, I never knew you!" (*Matthew* 7:21-23). They are the double-minded, neither hot nor cold, whom he spits from his mouth (*Revelation* 3:16).

3. We have witnessed the infestation of every institution with psychopaths—meaning those who can kill without remorse—while compassionate people and independent thinkers have been driven out.

Inference: Some are born psychopaths for they are Nephilim descendants bearing the mindset of rebellious angels. Others are conditioned to be psychopaths. How do you kill Conscience in large numbers of people? You get them to participate in rituals of atrocity.

All of this points to Freemasonry and other secret societies. According to Ben Bengtsson in *Medical Allusions in Freemasonry*, Red Cross founder Henry Dunant was a Freemason. So too were Anton Mesmer, who developed mesmerism, and Josef Guillotin, after whom the guillotine is named. Edward Jenner himself, pioneer of vaccines, was a Freemason.

As Below, so Above?

The poison attacking our lives and livelihoods drips from a poison tree producing poison fruit, but the root of that tree is a poisonous underground network of secret societies. That is why, on Apr. 11, 2024, I told a listening session of the U.S. negotiating team to the World Health Organization,...

> "You have exchanged the black robes of your secret societies with white coats and hospital scrubs, swapped

sacrificial knives with poison needles, blood-drenched altars with hospital beds, and you have desecrated your public oaths with secret oaths."

More on that encounter later. Meanwhile, the veil of secrecy over secret societies is getting thinner by the day as we spot them covering one eye, flashing hand signals, and exchanging Freemasonic handshakes.

This recalls the scoundrel and villain of *Proverbs* 6:12-15 "who winks with his eye,/ signals with his feet/ and motions with his fingers." The foot-signalling part is seen in their obsession with shoe symbolism, both in staging fake terrorism narratives and in Freemason initiation rituals.

Speaking of initiation, we do not give Freemason neophytes a pass with the excuse that they don't know what's going on at the 'adept' levels, for they have sworn an oath of atrocity at the very first level. As reported at evangelicaltruth.com, the initiate swears to secrecy "under no less a penalty than that of having my throat cut across, my tongue torn out by its roots, and buried in the rough sands of the sea at low-water mark."

Therefore, no Freemason can be trusted to keep any promise, not even marriage vows, for they will always defer to the requirements of their secret order, including covering for each other's crimes.

The Cult of Molech

And those crimes have been especially murderous towards children. I first realized this in 2021 when I heard Moderna was about to trial its COVID shot in six-month-old babies. "That's Molech worship!" I exclaimed, for Molech is the god of child sacrifice who plagued Israel whenever they forsook the Most High who brought them out of Egypt.

> "The Lord said to Moses, 'Say to the Israelites: Any Israelite or any foreigner residing in Israel who sacrifices any of his children to Molek is to be put to death. The members of the community are to stone him. I myself will set my face against him and will cut him off from his people; for by sacrificing his children to Molek, he has defiled my sanctuary and profaned my holy name. If the members of the community close their eyes when that man sacrifices one of his children to Molek and if they fail to put him to death, I myself will set my face against him and his family and will cut them off from their people, together with all who follow him in prostituting themselves to Molek.' "
>
> — *LEVITICUS* 20:1-5

Yet, even with the instinct that child sacrifice was the key motivation for COVID, I had no idea how bad things would get. In November 2021, under court order, Pfizer released its *Cumulative Analysis* report showing that among 28 potential babies of Pfizer-injected mothers, 26 died by spontaneous abortion and one by neonatal death among the known outcomes. There was only one normal delivery, and who knows if that child even survived beyond the reporting period?

The document was compiled from unsolicited adverse-event reports that Pfizer received between its initial 'emergency-use authorization' (EUA) in December 2020 and the close of February 2021. This meant, in Pfizer's own words, that "the magnitude of underreporting is unknown" (p.5).

And if these 'transplacental' harms did not kill the unborn, infants could die from the 'transmammary' harms of tainted breastmilk. If they somehow survived both of these, the deadly needle itself was ready to kill them as the FDA kept extending its EUAs for COVID injections to younger and younger age groups, finally reaching six-month-olds on June 17, 2022.

As investigative reporter Lara Logan observed at the time, "For them, the younger you are, the closer you are to God, the more pain they can inflict on God, so the more you can make a baby or a small child suffer, the greater your victory over God, and that is the only consideration for them."

Harvesting the Living to Prop up the Dead

Another ancient abomination to resurface these days is medical cannibalism. In *The Book of Jasher* which, like *First Enoch* is emerging as a pivotal text after centuries of suppression, we learn that the pharaoh who first enslaved the true Israelites (father to the pharaoh whom Moses defied and destroyed) was afflicted by sores all over his body. He smelt so bad that none could come near him. His physicians advised him to apply the fresh blood of a child to his wounds. To that end, a Hebrew child was kidnapped and sacrificed each day (76:25-62).

Today, the world is infested with such pharaohs and their Satanic priesthoods. Their atrocities include ritualized rape, torture, mutilation, murder, sacrifice, and live organ harvesting, especially against children. In the process, they collect and drink adrenochrome, the adrenalized blood of their terrorized and traumatized victims, to extend their lifespans and produce a more youthful appearance and, in the case of non-human entities and hybrids, to maintain their human disguise. Finally, there is full cannibalism as they eat the kosher child meat. Bodies and body parts and body products are their trade, their currency, their commodity, and their food. All this serves the Royal Secret of Freemasonry that, in the words of former Mason, Bill Schnoebelen, "you can live forever by sexually vampirizing children."

Does this sound far fetched to you, Brothers and Sisters? Nay, I have barely scratched the surface. As I have heard many survivors independently recount, the reality gets even worse, unimaginably so, and these atrocities are the underground root of a poison tree that poisons the world.

The Ninth Circle and 'King' Charles

In recent years, I have followed the work of Kevin Annett and the International Tribunal into Crimes of Church and State (ITCCS). On Oct. 6, 2025, the court issued arrest warrants against 13 members of the Ninth Circle secret society. The cult's name is taken from the Ninth Circle of Hell in Dante's epic poem, *Inferno*, which holds those who have betrayed a sacred trust, and membership is required for anyone wishing to become Pope, according to Annett.

Among the sentenced are: Charles Windsor (aka 'King Charles III'), Andrew Windsor (aka 'Prince Andrew'), Donald Trump, Albert Bourla (CEO of Pfizer), Mark Rutte (NATO secretary general and former prime minister of the Netherlands), and Robert Prevost (aka 'Pope Leo'), along with three Church of Rome cardinals.

The Court announced...

"1/ After a thorough examination of the evidence, the magistrates of the court have come to a unanimous verdict. The court finds all 13 of the primary defendants guilty as charged of complicity in crimes against humanity, murder, and participating in the trafficking and ritual rape, torture, and murder of children.

"2/ By a majority opinion, the court sentences all of the defendants in absentia to imprisonment for life, without the possibility of parole, and the forfeiture of their assets and authority. But in a dissenting opinion, two of the court magistrates state that the death penalty is required in the sentencing of those defendants who bear command responsibility for Ninth-Circle atrocities."

In an Oct. 5, 2025 interview, Kevin told broadcaster Shaun Attwood that the Court holds records of Ninth-Circle ceremonies dating back to 1869, along with eyewitness testimonies, affidavits, and video footage that "shows the very grizzly events of when these children are ritually killed, torn apart, cannibalized. That's all on video and photographic evidence which the court has and will be sharing with other courts and governments around the world."

'King' Charles.

These developments accord with my command to the very stones of castle, palace, chamber, tunnel, and dungeon, and to the very trees of groves, to tell the atrocities they have seen, including those by British royals. On Oct. 10, 1964, Queen Elizabeth II and Prince Philip abducted 10 native children from the Kamloops residential 'school' in Canada and attended a ceremony in which eight of those children were ritually slaughtered. The remaining two children, Cecilia Arnold and Edward Arnuse, both aged 10, were taken to Carnarvon Castle in Wales and ritually sacrificed on Oct. 30, 1964. This was when Prince Charles, nearing his 16th birthday, was initiated into the Ninth Circle. Kevin Annett reports,...

"Cecilia and Edward were ritually raped, tortured, killed, and cannibalistically devoured in the sub-basement crypt of Carnarvon Castle by a coven of the Vatican-led Ninth Circle cult. Present and participating that night in that blood feast were Philip Mountbatten-Windsor and his eldest son Charles, who was inducted into the cult that night: the man now called the King of England."

Fast forward from 1964 to 2010 when Charles issues a kill order against native man, William Arnold Combes, sole remaining eyewitness to the Kamloops abduction. On Feb. 24, 2011, Combes was forcibly detained by Canadian police in Vancouver, incarcerated against his will in St. Paul's Catholic Hospital, and murdered by arsenic poisoning. On Sept. 20, 2023, the chief prosecutor of the West Coast Common Law Court of Justice issued a Public Indictment against Charles et al stating,...

"On May 16, 2023, the Court received a sworn affidavit from a former army officer who for years was part of the British monarchy's security team. This officer states that in late December of 2010, he participated in a 'special operations' meeting in Buckinghamshire to plan the murder of William Combes. The meeting was called by Major Johnny Thompson of the Royal Regiment of Scotland, who was and remains the security advisor to the then-Prince of Wales and present 'King of England', Charles Mountbatten-Windsor."

Shocking as these revelations are, they barely begin to describe the breadth and depth of Luciferian crime that afflicts our nations. S.R.A., which stands for 'Satanic ritual abuse' (though 'Satanic ritual atrocity' would be more apt), is not the sole pastime of popes, princes, and politicians, but snakes its way through every town, city, and village, and into every human institution, and the Satanic ranking system that operates underground is not necessarily mirrored in the pecking order of official positions above ground.

The common characteristics of S.R.A., according to a *UK Column* transcript published in September 2015, include human sacrifice where children are forced to kill victims, eat their body parts, and drink human blood. They are forced to perform sex acts on each other, both to corrupt their innocence and to produce child pornography. Other tortures include shutting children in coffins and burying them alive. Prior to rituals, children are given hallucinogenic drugs. This interferes with their later recall of traumatic memories, a protection for the perpetrators.

Some children are kept in underground cages. Girls are forcibly impregnated, and the child is sacrificed after abortion or birth. "This adds new weight to the claim that abortion is the modern-day form of child sacrifice." The children are threatened with death to themselves, their loved ones, or their pets if they ever tell.

Brothers and Sisters, I acknowledge you may want to look away, but we who dwell in the shelter of the

Most High declare, decree, and resolve (and I invite you to say it with me)…

> that henceforth, no chamber, tunnel, dungeon, or crypt is deep enough or dark enough to hide these vipers and their crimes. From Heaven, we unmask them that they are unmasked on Earth, so that all shall know who they are and what they are and what they have done and whom they serve. So be it. So be it. And so be it.

"IT'S THE JEWS!"?

Humanity is shocked at the recital of the horrid cruelties which the Jews committed in the cities of Egypt, of Cyprus, and of Cyrene, where they dwelt in treacherous friendship with the unsuspecting natives… In Cyrene, they massacred 220,000 Greeks; in Cyprus 240,000; in Egypt a very great multitude. Many of these unhappy victims were sawed asunder.

— EDWARD GIBBON, *THE DECLINE AND FALL OF THE ROMAN EMPIRE*, VOL. 2

In 2025, I appeared several times on the *Maverick Artist* podcast of Victor-Hugo Vaca, Jr., but our partnership ceased after he escalated a minor and private disagreement into a public denouncement of me as a 'false prophet', putting reconciliation beyond reach. Until then, I had enjoyed our lively and spirited on-air conversations though I would wince when he said, "It's the Jews!" to explain everything. It was something of a mantra with him, and I jokingly suggested during one of my appearances that he emblazon it on a coat of many colours or train a parrot to say it or write a book titled, *It's the Jews!*

If I were to reduce the evils of this world to such a simplistic statement, I might say it's the secret societies, or the Nephilim descendants, or the Synagogue of Satan, but what does Scripture say?

The apostle Paul writes of "the Jews, who killed the Lord Jesus and the prophets and also drove us out. They displease God and are hostile to all men... they always heap up their sins to the limit" (*1 Thessalonians* 2:14-16).

Doesn't get any clearer than that, but then Jesus himself speaks of "those who are of the Synagogue of Satan, who claim to be Jews though they are not, but are liars" (*Revelation* 3:9). This suggests that it's *fake* Jews who are Satanic while *true* Jews are not.

Is something amiss with that translation? The *Contemporary English Version* has, "They claim to be God's people, but they are liars." *The Message* says, "... those who call themselves true believers but are nothing of the kind."

The vagaries of translation and even outright manipulation do muddy the waters sometimes in Bible study, requiring us to dig deeper and hear the Holy Spirit's witness. I recently read through the Old Testament *King James Version* and was struck by the sudden appearance of the word 'Jews' in *2 Kings* 16:6 to describe those who, until then, were referred to as 'Israel' or 'children of Israel' or 'Israelites' or simply 'people'. Who pulled this switcheroo?

A key question is, are we talking about a race or a religion, or both? In an article titled *The 'Jew' Problem is Anti-Semantic*, I ask,...

> "What is a 'Jew'? Is it someone who inhabits the Satanic state that has usurped the name of Israel? Is it a Hebrew? Is it someone who speaks Hebrew? Or someone who speaks Yiddish? Is it someone who believes in the Torah? Or is it someone who follows the abominations of the Talmud? Is it someone who is descended from the tribes of Israel? Or someone who is a descendant of the tribe of Judah? Is it someone defined by ritual, custom, or costume? Is it someone who wears a small hat, or a box on the forehead, or who kisses a wall? Is it someone who is descended from the Semites and is now being persecuted? In which case, Palestinians would be 'Jews'.
>
> "The whole thing is so fucking confusing that my head is spinning, and that, I suspect, is by design. Seems to me the word 'Jew' is a flag of convenience for every atrocity under the Sun. Given its vague and all-encompassing usage, it really means nothing at all."

On a personal level, I have acquaintances who call themselves Jews. They are not my enemies. They don't even know a spiritual battle is happening. I won't cut people out of my life just because they call themselves Jews whereas I have no hesitation in shunning eternally anyone who is a Freemason or in any other secret society. By their oaths alone, they have crossed a threshold of obscenity, made allegiance with a false god, and made themselves enemy to the Most High, to me, and to all Mankind.

Dustin Nemos was also a regular guest on the *Maverick Artist* podcast until, a few months after my departure, Victor-Hugo turned on him too. Dustin has made a career out of "naming the Jew" and says no-one does so more than he. He is also keen to point out physical traits that are markers of Nephilim descendants to this day, such as cone-shaped heads.

To which I caution, "men look at outward appearances, but the Lord looks at the heart" (*1 Samuel* 16:7); that "You shall know them by their fruits" (*Matthew* 7:16-20) rather than by labels; and that, when it comes time to sort the righteous from the spawn of Satan, as Jesus tells us in the parable of the wheat and the weeds, it will be primarily the work of angels to clean up that infernal mess (*Matthew* 13:37-43). These are among the reasons I continue to describe Satan's descendants and operatives as the Synagogue of Satan, a broad definition befitting a broad church.

Jews and Freemasonry

Yet it is instructive to examine the connection and overlap between secret societies and those who call themselves Jews. Here are some quotes that address this…

"Masonry is based on Judaism. Eliminate the teachings of Judaism from the Masonic ritual and what is left?"

— *JEWISH TRIBUNE*, OCT. 28, 1927
(VOL. 91, NO. 18)

"The influence of the Jewish Sanhedrin is today more powerful than ever in Freemasonry."

— O.B. GOOD, *THE HIDDEN HAND OF JUDAH*, 1936

"Each lodge is and must be a symbol of the Jewish temple; each Master in the Chair a representative of the Jewish King; and every Mason a personification of the Jewish workman."

— *AN ENCYCLOPEDIA OF FREEMASONRY*, 1906

"Masonry is a Jewish institution whose history, degrees, appointments, passwords, and explanations are Jewish from beginning to end."

— RABBI ISAAC WISE, *THE ISRAELITE OF AMERICA*, 1855

"Many people wonder aloud today, 'Freemasonry, is it Jewish?'... One thing is for sure: it is controlled behind the scenes by high-level Jewish interests."

— TEXE MARRS, *POWER OF PROPHECY* PRESENTATION

Many more quotes I could list, so the point is made. Symbols, too, support the argument, starting with the flag adopted by that fake state, government, and military that has usurped the name of 'Israel', the so-called 'Jewish State' that has squatted on stolen land in the Middle East since 1948.

This little beast that *claims* to represent Jews has as its flag the Star of Remphan, with six sides, six points, and six triangles. They call it 'the Star of David', but it is really the badge of Molech as described in Amos 5:26. "You have lifted up the shrine of Molech,/ the pedestal of your idols, the star of your god" (*Amos* 5:26).

And that symbol of abomination is venerated by Masons too. The Freemason lodge of Edinburgh, for example, has the Star of Remphan above its front door. Sometimes, it is combined with that other symbol of abomination, the Freemasonic Compass and Square.

A Potted History of the Seed War

What, then, is the historic connection between Freemasonry and those who call themselves Jews? This topic could fill many scholarly volumes, but that is not my aim here. This book is a weapon conceived and crafted to inflict devastating spiritual violence on enemies of the Most High, whatever colour, creed, flag, label, or disguise they wear, and they wear many. Therefore, brevity be the soul of my wit as I synthesize *The Curse of Canaan*, a book by Eustace Mullins, and video presentations by the late author and presenter, Texe Marrs.

We have already looked at the ancient enmity between the seed of Eve and the seed of the Serpent and called it the 'Seed War', and we have seen the Serpent's initial gambit of getting rebellious angels mating with the daughters of men, which spawned the Nephilim breed of giants and monsters. These infernal offspring were wiped out in the flood so that Noah and his sons, Shem, Ham, and Japheth, untainted in their genetic makeup, could repopulate the Earth without Nephilim pollution.

But there was a snag. Ham's wife was *not* pure in her genetics but, according to Mullins, a witch named Naamah, beautiful but cruel. Ham had four sons with her: Cush, Mizraim, Phut, and Canaan. Canaan's successors, the Canaanites, devoted themselves to demon worship, child sacrifice, and cannibalism, the word derived from combining 'Canaan' and 'Baal'. This breed "became the greatest curse upon humanity, and so they remain today," exemplifying "the Satanic urge to destroy civilization."

Cush, also a son of Ham and his witch, was father to Nimrod, founder of Babylon and builder of Babel, whose symbol is 'X'. Nimrod was heroically slain and beheaded by Shem, his grandfather's brother (lifespans were much longer in those days), after which Nimrod's priests had to take their hideous rites underground. That is the origin of Freemasonry, Mullins contends, which "aims for the extermination of life as we know it."

From the righteous line of Shem came Abraham, nine generations later (*Genesis* 11:10-26). Abraham was the father of Isaac, and Isaac begat Esau and Jacob, but Esau was another wayward brother who let the side down again by marrying Canaanite women (*Genesis* 36:2-3). This gave rise to the Edomites, purveyors of corrupt seed and vile deed, against whom the Most High "hath indignation for ever" (*Malachi* 1:4).

Jacob, whose name would change to Israel, had 12 sons, including Judah, who also let the side down by marrying Bathshua, a Canaanite princess (*Genesis* 38:2), an episode he later recounts in the apocryphal *Testament of Judah*.

> "And I knew that the race of the Canaanites was wicked, but the impulse of youth blinded my mind. And when I saw her pouring out wine, owing to the intoxication of wine I was deceived, and took her although my father had not counselled it."[1]

Of their three sons, one named Shelah survived, but Judah also had twin sons, Pharez and Zarah, with Tamar in the righteous line.[2]

Jacob's eleventh son, Joseph, was sold into slavery but eventually became Pharaoh's second in command in Egypt and brought his father and brothers there. At first, the true Israelites "were fruitful and multiplied greatly" in Egypt (*Exodus* 1:7), but a later pharaoh enslaved them and instigated a culling operation against their infant boys.

But Moses survived and, in his 80s, led the Israelites' exodus from Egypt. After his death, Joshua began a campaign of conquest against the Canaanite tribes inhabiting the Promised Land beyond the River Jordan.

The Most High commanded the Israelites to wipe out or drive out all the Canaanites in their path, and he forbade them to intermarry with that Satanic seed. If they failed in these commands, he warned, "then it shall come to pass that those ye let remain, of them shall be pricks in your eyes and thorns in your sides, and shall vex you in the land wherein ye dwell" (*Numbers* 33:55). The

Canaanite would "get up above thee very high, and thou shalt come down very low. He shall lend to thee, and thou shalt not lend to him" (*Deuteronomy* 28:43-44).

But fail they did. Although Joshua and his troops won many victories against the Canaanites, they didn't finish the job. The result was intermarriage and corruption with venomous seed, culminating in sacrifice of their own children to Molech.

The Pharisees.

Now, in this potted Bible history, we leap to John the Baptist's denouncement of the Pharisees and Sadducees as a "generation of vipers," even though he acknowledges they are descendants of Abraham (*Matthew* 3:7-9). He is not talking about an age group with that word, 'generation', but of ancestry, the poisoned and poison*ous* genetic code of Canaanites introduced through Esau's wives.

Jesus also acknowledges the Pharisees descend from Abraham (*John* 8:37) but tells them, "You belong to your father, the devil, and you want to carry out your father's desire" (*John* 8:44).

So the kinship between Satan and the Pharisees is based in genetics, not just shared ideas. Jesus despised these men, culminating in his scorching denouncements of them recorded in *Matthew* 23.[3]

So, is there a connection between the Pharisees of Jesus' time and the Jews of today? Yes, according to *Universal Jewish Encyclopedia* which states, "The Jewish religion, as it is today, traces its descent, without a break, through all the centuries, from the Pharisees" (p.474).

The Talmud and Other Satanic Texts

> *In law, what plea so tainted and corrupt,*
> *But, being seasoned with a gracious voice,*
> *Obscures the show of evil? In religion,*
> *What damned error, but some sober brow*
> *Will bless it and approve it with a text,*
> *Hiding the grossness with fair ornament?*
> *There is no vice so simple but assumes*
> *Some mark of virtue on his outward parts.*
>
> — WILLIAM SHAKESPEARE,
> THE MERCHANT OF VENICE, III.II.

A key reason for Jesus' disgust with the Pharisees was their "rules taught by men... the traditions of men" (*Mark* 7:7-8), otherwise known as 'the tradition of the elders'. At the time, it was an oral tradition but was later written down in a set of books collectively called the Talmud. Thus, "Pharisaism became Talmudism," to quote Rabbi Louis Finkelstein in his two-volume work, *The Pharisees*.

This Talmud is "the final word on Jewish rite and practice," according to an article by Rabbi Yossi Ives. It is also the basis of today's European Union if you believe its vampiric president, Ursula von der Leyen.

My overall impression from reading excerpts is that the Talmud is mostly the idle and incoherent ramblings of bored and boring rabbis with too much time on their hands. The Talmud collects their respective opinions but it doesn't always express their settled consensus.

My research also questions some of the claims I have heard about what the Talmud says. This could be because, like other evidence inconvenient to the powers that shouldn't be, some of the collection's most egregious abominations have been Memory-Holed from modern translations, but I did find within its dull prolixity the following (and put links in the electronic version of this book)…

> "An adult man who engaged in intercourse with a minor girl less than three years old has done nothing, as intercourse with a girl less than three years old is tantamount to poking a finger into the eye" (Ketubot 11b).

> "A descendant of Noah who engages in intercourse with the wife of another man in an atypical manner [anal] is exempt" from liability (Sanhedrin 58b).

> Intercourse with another man's wife is not punishable if she is dead, for "intercourse with a dead woman is not considered intercourse at all" (Yevamot 55b).

> "Adam had intercourse with each animal and beast in his search for his mate" (Yevamot 63a).

"The concept of licentiousness does not apply with regard to animals, as the payment for intercourse with a dog is not considered payment for prostitution" (Sotah 26b).

"If one set a dog against an individual and the dog killed him, or if one set a snake against an individual and the snake killed him, the one who set the dog or the snake is exempt from punishment" (Sanhedrin 78a).

"If one… intended to kill a gentile, for whose murder he is not liable to be executed in court, and he killed a Jew,… the assailant is exempt from execution, since his intent was to kill one for whose murder he is not liable" (Sanhedrin 78b).

" 'a life for a life' is not referring to execution; rather, the reference is to monetary restitution" (Sanhedrin 79a).

"… this ruling that permits the court to deceive a gentile is issued with regard to a regular gentile" (Bava Kamma 113b).

"A gentile who engages in Torah study is liable to receive the death penalty" (Sanhedrin 59a).

For Satan is a legalist, and likes to codify his tyranny in text, a trait we observe through his accomplices in parliaments, bureaucracies, and other corporations today.

The Torah, on the other hand, attributed to the authorship of Moses, comprises the first five books of the Old Testament. As E. Michael Jones warns in an April 2025 article, "it is through the Talmud that Rabbinic Judaism inverts, subverts, or perverts the Torah." He continues,…

> "There is no doubt that the Talmud presents a categorical attack on Christ. Talmudic theology stands firm in its complete and categorical rejection of Jesus Christ as the Messiah—a rejection that is both metaphysical and literal."

Rabbis today continue to assert Jewish supremacy—or 'loxism'—over the non-Jew, or 'Goy', and advocate atrocity against Christians. Among them is Yosef Mizrachi who asserts, "Even the Goy who bow down to an idol, who believe in JC, deserve death penalty."

The Kol Nidrei prayer.

Also among Satanic Jewish texts is the *Kol Nidrei prayer*, recited during the holiday of Yom Kippur, which declares all vows and oaths "null and void."

> "Let our vows not be considered vows; let our [self-imposed] prohibitions not be considered prohibitions; and let our oaths not be considered oaths."

The Kol Nidrei in English

The following is recited three times by the chazzan while the congregation follows along in an undertone:

כל נדרי All vows, [self-imposed] prohibitions, oaths, consecrations, restrictions, interdictions, or [any other] equivalent expressions of vows, which I may vow, swear, dedicate [for sacred use], or which I may proscribe for myself or for others, from this Yom Kippur until the next Yom Kippur which comes to us for good, [from now] we regret them all; all shall be hereby absolved, remitted, cancelled, declared null and void, not in force or in effect. Let our vows not be considered vows; let our [self-imposed] prohibitions not be considered prohibitions; and let our oaths not be considered oaths.

This abomination belongs in the same infernal fire as the secret oaths sworn by Freemasons and various secret-society scum who think that all other promises are disposable. Would you trust someone who thinks it is acceptable, or even commendable in the eyes of their god, to break a promise? Would you get into contract with them? Would you even trust your spouse's marriage vow?

These are just some of the Satanic texts venerated by 'Jews'. Also on that list are the *Kabbalah, Zohar, 'Noahide'* codes (call them not 'Laws'), *Protocols of the Learned Elders of Zion, Scofield Reference 'Bible'*, the *Balfour Declaration*, and the Egyptian *Book of the Dead*.

Jews and Genocide

Now, having looked at the Seed War and traced the Satanic bloodline through Canaanites and Pharisees, and witnessed the Satanic legal code enshrined in the Talmud and Yom-Kippur observances, we have context for genocides throughout the 20th century and continuing to this day.

In his video presentation, *Masonic Lodge Over Jerusalem*, Texe Marrs points out that the top-five founders of Communism in Russia, who "set records for bloodshed and bloodthirstiness... were, indeed, Jews, and all five were Freemasons." He noted too that, "the Jewish Masons who run Israel and to a great extent run the United States and Europe today, these men are no less bloodthirsty."

Gaza.

Today, we see Talmudic poison exuded through the inventive sadism of Israeli soldiers in Gaza, such as disguising grenades as cans of food to be picked up by starving children, tearing up homes of civilians, ritually raping prisoners, destroying civilian infrastructure, throwing pets from high buildings, and murdering patients in their hospital beds. Do we not by now have enough evidence to know them by their fruits and to regard the phrase 'Christian Zionism' as an oxymoron?

That soldiers commit such acts with gleeful abandon, even rejoicing in them through self-incriminating videos on social media, confirms we are looking at Molech-worshipping Nephilim spawn who are psychopaths from birth. The reason they do not have human traits of conscience and compassion is because they and their controllers are not human at all but descendants of giants and monsters, and they have grown up in a system that trains the population in psychopathy.

The ruling passions of Fake Israel are paranoia, jealousy, and hatred of the Creator, hatred of his creation, hatred of all that is noble, beautiful, and praiseworthy, and hatred of his image in us. To the extent that they outwardly resemble us, they hate themselves too. Yet they pretend to be true Israelites. In an inversion of Jacob pretending to be Esau (*Genesis* 27), they are Esau pretending to be Jacob, as observed by Bible scholar and author, Rob Skiba, who was medically murdered in 2021.

And speaking of medical murder, it is another weapon wielded by Fake Israel in service to Molech. In January 2022, the Anti-Defamation League (ADL)—whose job is to label as 'antisemitic' any critic of Fake Israel or of its war crimes or war criminals—gave its highest honour, the Courage Against Hate Award, to Albert Bourla, CEO of Pfizer. In December of that year, Prime Minister Netanyahu said in an interview, "Israel became, if you will, the lab for Pfizer."

Yet you may wonder why Fake Israel flaunts its genocidal military acts on social media while medical atrocities are kept hidden. Why are we subjected to a Satanic ritual of genocide porn as children are brutalized, burned, butchered, beheaded, and buried alive thousands of miles away, but we are not shown the ghastly spectacle of 'vaccine'-induced spontaneous abortions in our own countries, infants going into seizure at the breast of injected mothers, or breathing their last after a fatal injection themselves? Why? Because we have more agency to do something about the latter whereas we are deemed helpless onlookers of the former.

Jezebel's return.

The state of Israel and its inhabitants today bear no resemblance to the inheritance of Abraham, Isaac, and Jacob. For a true Christian, Israel is a place in the heart, not on a map, but the stolen territory called by this name today does echo the Israel once ruled by Ahab and Jezebel when child sacrifice was the state religion in worship of Baal.

I'm thinking too of how Jezebel had Naboth falsely accused and stoned to death so that Ahab could take over his vineyard, rip out the vines, and replace them with a vegetable garden (*1 Kings* 21). Similarly, Fake Israel today falsely accuses Palestinians, kills them, takes over their possessions, and uproots their olive trees. In service to this agenda, it created and continues to fund Hamas, "a Jewish terrorist group to blame the Palestinians so that they can kill all their children," to quote Dustin Nemos.

The royal couple's treachery towards Naboth goaded Elijah into confronting Ahab and decreeing his untimely death, along with the demise of all the sons in his line and of Queen Jezebel who would be fed to the dogs in the city of Jezreel. Of course, Satan's gang of accusers, such as the ADL, would label Elijah an 'antisemite' today just for denouncing the political leadership of Fake Israel.

Not that politicians elsewhere are much better. What a sickening spectacle on July 24, 2024 to see the puppets of Congress give some 50 standing ovations to Israeli prime minister Benjamin Netanyahu during a one-hour speech. A humiliation ritual, perhaps, and Satanic theatre from start to finish.

Meanwhile, at the time of writing, U.S. taxpayers are funding military atrocities against Palestinians; a Bill is before Congress that would revoke passports for critics of Fake Israel; and 250 American legislators are in Tel Aviv attending a '50-States-One-Israel' event and getting "guided programming."

Nor is it just the political system that's controlled by Fake Israel and its accomplices. It is banking, commerce, courts, media and social media, medicine, militaries, movies, music, porn, publishing, and more. Mainstream churches, too, prostrate themselves before it.

All this is written in the annals of infamy. Since the flood, the Nephilim descendants have never been purged again but have spread their filthy ways throughout the Earth. Upon them, says Jesus, is "all the righteous blood shed on Earth, from the blood of righteous Abel to the blood of Zechariah son of Berechiah, whom you murdered between the temple and the altar" (*Matthew* 23:35).

Yes, from Abel to Zechariah, their crimes are the A to Z of abomination, assassination, atrocity, cannibalism, cruelty, deception, desecration, destruction, dispossession, election-rigging, enslavement, false-flag, famine, genocide, infanticide, infiltration, injustice, lie, massacre, mutilation, perversion, plague, poisoning, pollution, propaganda, rape, revolution, sadism, terrorism, theft, torture, treason, and war. In short, every conceivable harm. They are not just 'bad people', they are Satan's bloodline, a devil's brood, wearing the outward disguise of Mankind. Of course, they hate and target true Christians above all.

Then, add usury to the list with a debt-based financial system that continues to extort us. This plays out the warning I quoted before that the Canaanite "shall lend to thee, and thou shalt not lend to him" (*Deuteronomy* 28:43-44).

Imagine I could write numbers on bits of paper and then make you work for them, and then claw back most of what you earned through fines, fees, taxes, debt, inflation, and property confiscation. I could also bribe every mover and shaker without consequence while paying off vicious cops and judges and other compliant order-followers. I could force people into debt and all manner of slavery—wage slavery, debt slavery, medical slavery, prison slavery, sex slavery, and finally digital slavery. Meanwhile, I could buy up real assets, drive up rents and taxes, and make the basics of life unaffordable for everyone else. I would inflict mass homelessness then criminalize the homeless so that I could herd them into camps as slave labour to be worked to death or disappeared. If I did all that, Brothers and Sisters, you would rightly consider me a son of Hell, yet that is what the Canaanites and Edomites have done, are doing, or are planning to do to us.

The inherent cruelty of a Canaanite is implacable. No argument will persuade it nor petition dissuade it; no act of mercy will soften it nor moral code reform it. It cannot be reasoned with and cannot be taught. It will not honour a promise or contract it makes with you, it will secretly despise any public oath it makes, and you can be sure it will not reciprocate any act of kindness you show it. It is a psychopath, incapable of empathy, and the only solution is to destroy it, as surely as David destroyed the six-fingered giant Goliath then cut off his head to make sure.

Yet, for lack of this knowledge, Mullins writes, the descendants of Shem perish. They "have never understood their peril, and they have frequently been subject to massacre because their essential goodness made it impossible for them to believe the vileness of the Canaanites."

To quote a brilliant meme I saw recently, "Some of you would've told David to pray for Goliath. And not to cause a scene." But, if all the world's a stage, and we are actors on it, then causing a scene is what we're here to do! Jesus caused a scene when he drove the moneychangers from the temple and when he healed a man on the Sabbath.

After which, "the Pharisees went out and began to plot with the Herodians how they might kill Jesus" (*Mark* 3:6). The Herodians were the political operatives of Herod Antipas, the local ruler appointed by Rome, so the conspiracy of Pharisee and Herodian was also the Satanic alliance of synagogue and state. It continues to this day and with Rome's connivance, led by a yarmulke-wearing pope.

In Summation

I asked earlier if we meant a race or a religion when talking about self-professing 'Jews'. It is both. Satan's offspring have developed a Satanic religion and codified it with Satanic texts, a practice they continue through legislation today.

It is therefore righteous and godly to be racist against these Nephilim/Canaanite/Edomite spawn, though they are not really a 'race' as the word is used today, more of a breed whose very genetics are a poison to Mankind. I am therefore 'breedist' against them in accordance with the Holy Spirit.

Is it the 'Jews'? I don't even know what the word means, but if you're talking about Nephilim bloodlines, Canaanites, Edomites, Talmudists, Zionists, secret societies, and observers of Yom Kippur and the *Kol Nidrei* prayer, then yes, it is the Jews. It is not 'anti-Semitic' to denounce them; it is righteous and godly, for they are the real anti-Semites who, according to their ancient grudge, hate, attack, and murder the descendants of Shem.

TRAITOR TRUMP

In a Nov. 13, 2020 speech, during his first term in the White House, Donald J. Trump called 'Operation Warp Speed', "The single greatest mobilization in U.S. history, pioneering, developing, and manufacturing therapies and vaccines in record time. Numbers like nobody has seen before."

In an era of common sense, that statement alone would disqualify him from ever coming near public office again, but here we are heading into 2026 during a second term. In recent years, I have compiled some 30 questions about Trump, aimed especially at his supporters, which none has attempted to answer. If they did, I doubt they'd get past the first question: Did Trump, on the campaign trail in 2016, say he would bring back "a hell of a lot worse than waterboarding?" (Waterboarding is a form of torture where they bring someone to the verge of drowning, repeatedly.)

Yes he did, desecrating the Eighth Amendment's prohibition of "cruel and unusual punishment." Again, in any sane society, this would bar Trump eternally from holding office. So would his many blasphemous words and deeds, such as calling himself 'The Chosen One', or appropriating the title 'Prince of Peace' when, on Feb. 26, 2024, the Israel Heritage Foundation named him so as it gave him a menorah representing "the eternal light of the world."

So let me remind you of a prophecy in *Daniel*...

"There shall arise a king of shameless countenance, wise in dark speakings. He shall be mighty and strong, but not in his own strength. He shall destroy above measure, and all he goeth about shall prosper, and he shall slay the holy people. And through his policy, falsehood shall prosper. His heart shall be proud, and by peace he shall destroy many. He shall stand up against the Prince of princes, yet he will be destroyed though not by human hand."

— 8:23-35

Is it a contradiction that many could be destroyed by peace? Not when you consider that one-world government is a kind of peace, though it's not the kind of peace you or I would want to live under. Trump's brand of peace was also on display when he addressed the Israeli parliament ('Knesset') on Oct. 13, 2025 and received standing ovations of his own. Following yet another fake ceasefire in Gaza, he told the Israeli worthies in a long, grandiose, and characteristically boastful speech,...

"the sun rises on a holy land that is finally at peace, a land and a region that will live, God willing, in peace for all eternity... and because of us, the enemies of all civilization are in retreat, thanks to the bravery and incredible skill of the Israeli Defense Forces... Israel, with our help, has won all that they can by force of arms. You've won. I mean, you've won. Now it's time to translate these victories against terrorists on the battlefield into the ultimate prize of peace and prosperity for the entire Middle East. It's about time you were able to enjoy the fruits of your labor."

Thus, in Trump's mind, Israel wins peace and prosperity by force of arms, echoing the Party slogans of Orwell's *1984*: "War is peace. Freedom is slavery. Ignorance is strength." Trump also hailed the Abraham Accords and announced an "unbelievably popular... Board of Peace."

His logic echoes my favourite example of irony, one I shared often with my students when teaching English literature: "And, waving our red weapons o'er our heads,/ Let's all cry, 'Peace, freedom, and liberty!' " (Shakespeare, *Julius Caesar*, III.i.) Bear in mind too the apostle Paul's warning that, "While people are saying, 'Peace and Safety,' destruction will come on them suddenly" (*1 Thessalonians* 5:3).

Trump even managed to squeeze some sorcery into his speech, telling the assembly, "I flew to Iraq and I met with a man named Caine. I said, 'What's your first name?' He said, 'They call me 'Raizin', sir.' I say, 'Wait a minute. Your name is Raizin Caine? I've been looking for you for a long time. You gotta be kidding.' "

The Magic Bullet of Butler

Consider, too, the ridiculous pantomime of a botched assassination attempt on Trump in Butler, Pennsylvania on July 13, 2024. I have worked as a stage actor and have some training in stage combat where you always inflict a pretend injury on the upstage side—the side the audience cannot see. So it was with the purported injury to Trump's ear. As for the live audience sitting behind Trump, their indifference to the bullets supposedly flying around them suggests they were paid extras on the umpteenth take and bored by the whole exercise.

And what about Trump turning his head at just the right moment to avoid death? Consider how long he took pointing to the billboard on his right and repeating himself before those shots rang out. It was a theatrical cue, but the stage managers were late with the sound of bullets, requiring Trump to extemporize. Then there were those chubby girls supposedly in the Secret Service who fumbled their weapons as they reholstered them. They were extras, and inadequately trained in stage combat.

I refer you to the exemplary work of Ole Dammegard for granular analysis of the false-flag fakery of Butler, Pennsylvania and other terrorism spectacles, but I have given you my insights from an actor's point of view. Which missing letter did you think of first in the above photo?

Make-believe Christians.

After the Butler deception was perpetrated, it was time to milk the narrative of Divine Providence protecting Trump and to get Christians believing it. Among the duped was Mike Adams, most ignorant of what he's most assured, who said on July 15, 2024, just two days after the event, "It was by the grace of God that bullet missed Trump's skull" (at 48:55). No, Mike, the grace of God had nothing to do with it. It was all theatre, and you fell for it. Meanwhile, the Illuminati impresarios surrounded Trump with a counterfeit-holy entourage of make-believe Christians giving thanks for the purported miracle.

This is straight out of Shakespeare's *Richard III*. Richard, Duke of Gloucester, has killed everyone standing between him and the throne of England, but he lacks public support to take the crown. His henchman, Buckingham, therefore arranges to bring a delegation to his quarters and beg Richard to become King, having privately coached him beforehand to…

> *get a prayer-book in your hand,*
> *And stand betwixt two churchmen, good my lord;*
> *For on that ground I'll build a holy descant.*
>
> — III.VII.

The ploy works, and a tyrant is installed, and it has worked again this time on the feeble-minded. Among Trump's sycophants was that lying piece of shit, 'Pastor' Brandon Biggs, who outlined the planned events of Butler months beforehand and tried to present the planning as prophecy. The gullible swallowed the deception and hailed Trump their saviour.

Biggs also predicted his man would be "on fire for Jesus" after the ordeal. If that were so, Trump would fall to his knees in repentance and beg for forgiveness for unleashing mass destruction on the peoples of the States and of the world.

On the contrary, Trump has doubled down on his atrocities, including secret ones. In an Oct. 14, 2025 update on Ninth-Circle prosecutions, Kevin Annett told *The Imagination Podcast* that Keith Schiller, a former bodyguard to Trump and head of White-House security during his first term, saw Trump "at a snuff film and sacrifice of a young Asian girl about five years old at Epstein's apartment in Manhattan in the spring of 1999."[1]

Thus, combined in that Satanic entity known as Donald J. Trump are the embodiments of Freemason, Talmudic Jew, ritual child sacrifice, medical genocide, military genocide, and the 'King of Fierce Countenance' in end-times prophecy, also known as 'Little Horn'.

Your Trump Quiz

Here, then, is the full Trump quiz. Some of the questions have a factual answer: did such a thing happen or not? Others will be questions of inference: if such a thing happened, what does it mean? So after each question, I will specify whether it is a question of "Fact" or "Inference." Ready?

1. Did Trump, on the campaign trail in 2016, say he would bring back "a hell of a lot worse than waterboarding?" *Fact.*

2. Does the Eighth Amendment to the *Constitution* prohibit "cruel and unusual punishment"? *Fact.*

3. Is waterboarding cruel? *Inference.*

4. Is Trump familiar with the *Constitution*? *Inference.* Has he even *read* the *Bill of Rights*? *Inference.*

5. Did Trump say in a Nov. 13, 2020 speech that he was "very proud" of Operation Warp Speed and that he "had tremendous help from the military" in bringing it about? *Fact.* Has he recanted or repented since? *Fact.*

6. Did Trump unilaterally withdraw from the Intermediate Nuclear Forces treaty with Russia in 2019? *Fact*

7. Did this put the world in greater danger of nuclear annihilation? *Inference.*

8. In December 2020, did Trump pardon mercenaries who slaughtered civilians in Nisour Square, Iraq? *Fact.*

9. Did Trump fail to pardon Edward Snowden? *Fact.*

10. Did Trump continue the persecution of Julian Assange? *Fact.*

11. Does the First Amendment to the *Constitution* enshrine Freedom of the Press? *Fact.*

12. A repeat of Question 4. Is Trump familiar with the *Constitution*? *Inference.* Has he even *read* the *Bill of Rights*? *Inference.*

13. Did Trump announce, on the campaign trail in 2016, implementation of a "biometric entry-exit visa tracking system"? *Fact.*

14. Does the Fourth Amendment to the *Constitution* enshrine our Right to be secure in our persons, houses, papers, and effects from unreasonable searches and seizures? *Fact.*

15. A repeat of Questions 4 and 12. Is Trump familiar with the *Constitution*? *Inference.* Has he even *read* the *Bill of Rights*? *Inference.*

16. Did Trump, on June 1, 2020 brandish a Bible in front of St. John's Church in D.C.? *Fact.*

17. Was this an act of blasphemy? *Inference.*

18. On Feb. 26, 2024, did the Israel Heritage Foundation hail Trump 'the Prince of Peace' as it gifted him a menorah representing "the eternal light of the world"? *Fact.* Did Trump refuse the gift or the title? *Fact.*

19. Was *this* an act of blasphemy? *Inference.*

20. Did Trump announce, in a Feb. 4, 2025 press conference with Benjamin Netanyahu, his intention to "level" Gaza? *Fact.*

21. Did this support ongoing atrocity and genocide against Palestinian peoples? *Inference.*

22. Did Trump call for the death penalty for 'anti-Semitism'? *Fact.*

23. Does the First Amendment to the *Constitution* enshrine Freedom of Speech and of the Press? *Fact.*

24. A repeat of Questions 4, 12, and 15. Is Trump familiar with the *Constitution*? *Inference.* Has he even *read* the *Bill of Rights*? *Inference.*

25. In July 2025, did Trump sign the so-called *GENIUS Act* by which a federal agency can "seize, freeze, burn, or prevent the transfer of payment" of anyone who doesn't obey Government decrees or who questions the latest propaganda? *Fact.*

26. Does the Bible warn in *Daniel* 8:23-25 of a man of fierce countenance who will consider himself superior? *Fact.*

27. Does Trump consider himself superior? *Inference.*

28. Does the same passage in *Daniel* warn that the man "by peace will destroy many."? *Fact.*

29. Does *Revelation* alert us to a head who seemed to have a fatal wound but recovers from it (13:3)? *Fact.*

30. Is the "fatal wound" an assassination attempt? Is it a restoration to power after a stolen election? *Inference.*

Recently, when browsing on Rumble, I saw an advertisement for a "Trump gold coin," featuring Trump's stern-faced mugshot. (And that's not me calling it a mugshot; it's the advertisement.)

I initially thought it must be a gold ounce which

would sell for thousands of dollars. I click the link to see it's priced at $19.95, so obviously not a gold coin, just a gold-*colored* coin. Big difference!

Similarly, is Trump gold-plated, gold-colored, counterfeit, fool's gold, a gold shade of orange, or just some bright shiny thing? *Inference*.

THE DECEPTION-INDUSTRIAL COMPLEX

Butler, Pennsylvania was a huge and elaborate deception, to my eyes and to the eyes of other brothers and sisters in Christ, a clumsy, blundering, and inept stage production with more plot holes than a termite's nest. The same goes for all manner of spectacular acts of terrorism orchestrated by the Illuminati impresarios throughout history, including 9/11 of course, where even some mainstream media outlets are now beginning to question, however tentatively, the official narrative.

I was in New York City at the time and initially went through the intended emotions of rage and revenge, but came to realize over the following months that the official story didn't add up, that it was a plot device to conjure more enemies abroad and more tyrannical legislation at home. Orwell warned us about such false-flag tactics back in 1949 with his dystopian novel, *1984*....

"The proles, normally apathetic about the war, were being lashed into one of their periodical frenzies of patriotism. As though to harmonize with the general mood, the rocket bombs had been killing larger numbers of people than usual... Once when he [Winston] happened in some connection to mention the war against Eurasia, she [Julia] startled him by saying casually that in her opinion the war was not happening. The rocket bombs which fell daily on London were probably fired by the Government of Oceania itself, 'just to keep people frightened.' "

False flags and psyops are a huge industry populated by crisis actors and crisis extras. I exposed one of them, Kayla McDonald, an actress pretending to be a registered nurse for vaccination propaganda put out by Intermountain Healthcare in 2021. More recently, I realized that David Cole Wheeler, with whom I played Shakespeare in New York City, pretended to be a grieving father for the Sandy Hook Shooting hoax in 2012. He did so better than his second Sandy-Hook role as a military sniper, at which he was deliciously inept.

I go into more detail about both of these in the Extras section below, but these examples just scratch the surface of the crisis-acting industry. Why couldn't these mediocre talents fail gracefully like the rest of us, instead of scrounging rotten crumbs from the casting director's table?!

As I said, Butler, Pennsylvania was a farce, yet it

managed to convince millions that Trump was their champion against a treacherous Deep State who wanted him out of the way.

No, Trump *is* the Deep State, and the job of the so-called Democrats in the election campaign of 2024 was to fall on their swords by mounting their weakest, least qualified, and most ridiculed candidate in Kamala Harris. Then, once the Party had imploded, Trump could become king of a one-party state serving a one-world government.

Of course, we already had a de facto one-party state anyway, a uniparty, in which Republicans and Democrats, while loudly contending on trivial matters, would collaborate to install a dictatorship and perpetuate war, but Trump's role is to be the final nail in the nation's coffin, even while he is portrayed as a Messianic saviour figure.

The White-Tile Team

Which brings me to what I call the White Tile Team, a term I have coined from the alternating black and white tiles of a Freemason floor. The black tiles are easy to spot. Take for instance, Klaus Schwab, who founded the World Economic Forum, that infernal think-tank where a dystopian future is celebrated, Man merged with machine, and everyone chipped with mind-controlling software. Then there's his lizard side-kick, Yuval Noah Harari, who relishes the idea of "surveillance under the skin" and regards humans as "hackable animals."

The black-tile politicians, too, are easy to spot, such as former Canadian prime minister, Justin Trudeau, who seized so-called emergency powers in 2022 to crush dissent when truckers opposed his medical tyranny; or Jacinda Ardern who, when prime minister of New Zealand, terrorized the people and claimed that side effects from COVID shots were "a sign that the vaccine's doing what it should." Then there's that Eurodalek, Ursula von der Leyen, who declares, "A better world also means a healthier world, and vaccination is our best chance to do this."

These black-tile operatives cast word-spells such as, "You will own nothing and be happy." It is not prophecy, for that which comes out of the mouth of false prophets is, by definition, false prophecy. It could be forecast based on planning, or it could be mere speculative fantasy, but the idea is to get people repeating it to magnify the spell and give it more currency, a form of witchcraft.

In any case, the job of these black-tile operatives is to terrify us with dystopian prediction and threat so that the white tiles can enter the scene, false heroes offering token opposition to tyranny while strenuously avoiding the bigger picture and siphoning off dissent into manageable forums or 'Limited Hangouts'. These are the false prophets and wolves in sheep's clothing Jesus warned us about. Their platforms are mysteriously well funded and enjoy viewing figures far exceeding their charisma or talent. They'll tell you some of what you want to hear but, being whitewashed tombs, they cannot conceal their spiritual death stench or 'musk' from those with discernment. In the words of Sir Escanor,...

> "The same people signing the checks are the ones scripting the outrage. The same hands building the cage are the ones posing as freedom fighters.... Hope for sale. And let's wait it out and see. All wrapped in patriotism, truth and justice, detox kits, alternative health merch, and the illusion of independence."

I close with this admonition to 'truthers' that Jesus is *the* Way, *the* Truth, and *the* Life (*John* 14:6), so if your search for Truth culminate not in him, you are susceptible to deceptions more subtle and insidious than the more obvious lies. As one BitChute viewer warned in comment on a video by Jeff Berwick in October 2025,...

> "Jesus Christ is not part of your escape plan—He IS the plan. He's not a patch on your ideology—He's the only Way, Truth, and Life. And unless a man is born again—not awakened by Bitcoin or psychedelics or anarchy, but by the spirit of God—he shall not see the Kingdom. Let this be a warning to all who have followed voices like Jeff's. His doctrine is another gospel, and his 'truth movement' is part of the Beast's strategy to lead you everywhere but the Cross."

As for those who say they are "awake" or have "woken up," what are you waking up to? "Awake, O sleeper, and arise from the dead, and Christ shall shine his light on you" (*Ephesians* 5:14). If you wake not to him, you are in another level of sleep. Similarly, if you consider yourself one of the 'Freedom Movement', know that, "If the son sets you free, you will be free indeed" (*John* 8:36). Otherwise, you are in a subtler form of slavery.

THE CHRISTIAN'S AUTHORITY IN SPIRITUAL WARFARE

This is the chapter on which all the others hinge. We, sons of Eve, are now at the front lines of battle, pressing on until we have crushed the head of the Serpent, and the Serpent strikes no more. In readiness for this battle, our mighty Captain and Saviour has equipped us with "authority to trample on snakes and scorpions and to overcome all the power of the enemy" (*Luke* 10:19), and the God of Peace will soon crush Satan under our feet (*Romans* 16:20).

Yet some qualities of the serpent we may emulate, for Jesus instructs us to be "wise as serpents" (*Matthew* 10:16). Remember, too, that when Moses and his brother Aaron come to Pharaoh's court and issue their demands, Aaron demonstrates prophetic authority by throwing down his staff, and it turns into a snake. Pharaoh's sorcerers imitate the act, but Aaron's snake eats their snakes (*Exodus* 7:8-12).

I have recalled this scene many times in my writings about the COVID era because the so-called vaccines are like the serpents of Pharaoh, and we of prophetic calling have overthrown them with the word of our testimony. I also observe how the non-venomous indigo snake makes easy work of overpowering and devouring rattlesnakes, another representation of our victory over Molech's medical cult. If you have the stomach for it, you can find videos of these one-sided snake battles on line.

Moses went on to annihilate Pharaoh and his chariots and his million-man army, not with a sword but by prophetic utterance. He was operating in an arena above the conventional battlefields of men…

> "For we wrestle not against flesh and blood, but against principalities, against powers, against the rulers of the darkness of this world, against spiritual wickedness in high places."
>
> — *EPHESIANS* 6:12

> "For though we live in the world, we do not wage war as the world does. The weapons we fight with are not the weapons of the world. On the contrary, they have divine power to demolish strongholds."
>
> — *2 CORINTHIANS* 10:3-4

Binding and Loosing

Spiritual warfare comes with the territory for those who are in Christ, and we need only take him at his word to prevail. Along with having authority to overcome all the power of the enemy, we also have authority to bind and loose…

> "Whatsoever you bind on Earth is bound in Heaven. Whatsoever you loose on Earth is loosed in Heaven."
>
> — *MATTHEW* 18:18

The implications are staggering, and will make our enemies stagger. Think of the world-changing effects when we bind in prayer,…

- The flow of funds to organizations and institutions and individuals who are trying to destroy us.

- The flow of poisons issued by Big Pharma.

- The flow of adrenochrome, that substance allegedly extracted from tortured children and consumed by tyrants to seek a more youthful appearance.

- Live organ harvesting.

... and when we loose in prayer,...

- The history and technology and land masses that have been hidden from us.

- Books in the Vatican Library and artefacts in museum vaults that are inconvenient to official history.

- The masks and disguises of people and entities pretending to be what they're not.

Speaking Truth *to* Power, Not Just *About* Power

Our exemplar in binding and loosing is Elijah. He commanded the rain to cease and the rain to fall, unleashed fire from Heaven, and shut down the lives of kings. He is also our exemplar of speaking Truth to Power. He embodies Christ's observation that "The Kingdom of Heaven has been advancing forcefully (violently), and forceful men lay hold of it" (*Matthew* 11:12).

Nowadays, when people talk of speaking Truth to Power, they usually mean speaking Truth *about* Power to each other. But not Elijah, who repeatedly got in Power's face. We see this when he confronts Ahab over his treachery against Naboth and tells the king that every son of his line, "everyone who pisses against a wall," will be wiped out, their corpses fed to the crows in the country and to the dogs in the city. Jezebel herself would be dogs' meat (*1 Kings* 21).

Ahab went on to die in battle, his son Ahaziah died after a drunken fall, Jezebel was pushed from a balcony and her body devoured by dogs at the wall of Jezreel, and Jehu slaughtered Ahab's remaining sons and had their severed heads brought to him in baskets (*2 Kings* 10).

And it wasn't just the political establishment that crumbled before Elijah. He famously demolished the religious order by putting to death several hundred false prophets of Baal on Mount Carmel (*1 Kings* 18), and he brought Israel's military order literally to its knees after calling down fire on two detachments of soldiers sent to apprehend him. "If I'm a man of God, let fire descend from Heaven and consume thee and thy men!" (*2 Kings* 1). And so it did. Elijah's successor, Elisha, also made and unmade kings, and overthrew armies by prophetic decree.

> *For what can armour, helmet, sword, or shield*
> *In that arena do where prophets wield*
> *Their power, and works of angels are unsealed?*
> *This is a battle of another field!*
>
> — A. LEROY, *ELIJAH: A FICTIONAL REINVENTION OF THE GREAT PROPHET'S LIFE IN A 12-PART EPIC POEM*

Today, we of prophetic authority are called again to

destroy false-hearted politicians, praetorians, and priests. You have probably seen video clips of enraged citizens shouting at tyrant psychopaths such as Bill Gates. "You're a murderer, Bill Gates!" shouts one. "You belong in jail, Bill Gates!" shouts another.

True statements, but without prophetic authority. How much more powerful to declare in their faces,...

> "From Heaven, I unmask you that you are unmasked on Earth, so that all shall know who you are and what you are and what you have done and whom you serve."

Or,...

> "From Heaven, I decree your downfall and destruction that you are destroyed on Earth."

I acknowledge that our adversaries often surround themselves with protective bubbles of security personnel, along with various gatekeepers and go-betweens to filter their calls, letters, and emails, in which case I devise a way to cut through. For example, if I am sending a letter to some figurehead and it will likely be looked at first by one of their staff, I begin with, "Destruction befalls any who impedes this message to...".

Speaking Truth to police officers.

Between taking down the big targets, we're likely to

have run-ins with so-called police. They should be *peace* officers, keepers of the Peace, and impartial between opposing parties. In the case of British officers, they should be keeping their Constable's Oath of "upholding fundamental human rights," while those in the States should be defending with their lives the Rights enshrined in the *Bill of Rights,* including the Right to be secure in our persons, houses, papers, and effects, as set out in the Fourth Amendment.

What do we see instead? Banditry, threat and intimidation, road piracy, outright theft, and extreme violence. In the words of @mrbeaker8188, commenting on a YouTube video, the playbook of police today is, "Instigate, Escalate, Intimidate, Fabricate, Retaliate." They have zero regard for their oaths, and for the most part serve instead secret oaths sworn to secret societies.

And they are as stupid as they are brutal, making up rules as they go and lying when challenged on the illegality and unlawfulness of their behaviour. They have become mere order followers in the enforcement of corporate policy that has nothing to do with True Law, doing the bidding of Satanic monsters just so they can collect a paycheck.

How to deal with these fuckwits? First, the battle is won in the mind. Know, therefore, that we have authority over police, that we are the Law to *them*, and we are the ones issuing 'lawful orders' to *them*. Again, I quote from the documentary *Strawman*...

> "Government is a creation of Man, and a creation of Man can never have authority over Man."

Same goes for every other man-made institution, not just police but courts too. We as Living Men and Living Women have authority over all of them.

It is gratifying to see videos of well-informed men humiliating power-tripping cops, especially the road-pirate variety who want to meet revenue targets by extorting motorists. Even so, I rarely see anyone fully exercise their logical authority, let alone combine it with spiritual authority.

There is no one-size-fits-all approach when dealing with would-be enforcers, of course, but here are some weapons at our disposal, especially in Britain and the States United...

1. Get their names and badge numbers.

2. Demand proof they are who they say they are, to make sure they are not impersonating police officers. Merely wearing a uniform will not suffice. Insist they show you government-issued photo ID.

3. Ask them if they have sworn a public Oath, such as the Constable's Oath in Britain, which promises to uphold "fundamental human rights," and ask if they are acting under their

Oath now. Tell them to recite it. Or if you are in the States, tell a cop to recite the Fourth Amendment. If they can't, you are entitled to arrest them and put them on trial in a Common-Law court for dereliction of duty.

4. Ask them if they have sworn a secret oath to a secret society. If so, they have desecrated their public Oath. As Jesus said, you cannot serve two masters (*Matthew* 6:24). They will love their secret oath and hate their public Oath. The dual-oath swearers are eternally condemned; they are the spat out (*Revelation* 3:15-16) and the never known (*Matthew* 7:22-23).

5. If they ask you whether you "understand," you answer, "No," for you do not stand under them.

6. Remember you have the Right to Remain Silent and not to answer questions.

7. They may call a statute or ordinance 'law', but it isn't. Only God makes Law, and Man makes legislation, and even that is too grandiose a term for their tyrant code. All the legislatures that conjured it are corporations, and corporations can only write company policy that applies to their employees and to no-one

else. Same goes for all their regulations, procedures, ordinances, and executive orders. Without our signed consent, these fictions have no more authority to compel us than a knife trying to wound the wind or stab water.

8. You are not in Contract with these dickheads or their dickhead masters. If they cite some statute, have them show it to you, and if they come up with something, ask them where you signed it!

9. Also remember Presumption of Innocence. Just because some cop thinks you look suspicious doesn't allow them to violate your Rights. You are innocent 'til proven guilty, not the other way around. If they detain you or inconvenience you without saying what crime they suspect you of, they are perpetrating an unlawful arrest.

10. Even a *threat* to arrest you because you won't comply with some unconstitutional demand, or to bring violence against you or damage or confiscate your property, is an unlawful arrest.

11. If they attempt a search or seizure, or ask for your ID, ask them to produce a Warrant.

12. If they invent some crime, ask who the victim is, for where there is no victim, there is no crime. Who is bringing an allegation against you? Where is the signed statement or affidavit testifying against you?

13. By now, you will be able to list several examples where the badge tyrants have broken True Law. You may want to cite *Magna Carta*, which applies in the States United via the Ninth Amendment (that safeguards all pre-existing Rights): "We will appoint as justices, constables, sheriffs, and bailiffs only men who know the law and are minded to keep it well" (Article 45). Since the enforcers have proven by now that they do *not* know the Law and are *not* minded to keep it well, they are in dereliction of duty and can be arrested and put on trial in a Common-Law court.

14. I am not saying that a constitution is Law, nor is a bill of Rights, nor even *Magna Carta*. Only the Creator can make Law, and Man cannot touch that realm, but it *is* Law to would-be enforcers because they are contractually bound to it by public Oath. You can also cite statutes and court precedents on the rare occasions they contain language beneficial or protective for us.

15. Follow up with, "He who breaks the Law is under a curse—*Deuteronomy* 27:26." Describe a curse that will befall them such as, "If you fail to follow *my* lawful orders, you will not have a moment's joy for the rest of your life and, in the life to come, you will have eternal torment. Now, would you like to reconsider your position today?"

16. If they don't back off, unleash! "From Heaven, I decree your downfall and destruction, that you are destroyed on Earth, never to trouble me or anyone else ever again."

17. Add other punishments as you see fit: "You will not eat though your plate is full; you will not sleep though your bed is soft,"... etc.

18. Finally, there is the Elijah option, as he unleashed against the costumed enforcers of Jezebel, "If I'm a man of God, let fire descend from Heaven and consume thee and thy men!" (*2 Kings* 1:12)

Brothers and Sisters, there is such a target-rich environment of easily identifiable tyrants before us that we can all find opportunity to speak Truth *to* Power using our own form of spiritual word-violence. This is to strike in the arena were we are strongest, as opposed to physical violence where our enemies have weaponry and budgets we can never match.

My argument against using physical violence ourselves is therefore a purely practical one, not a moral one, in that it would play to our enemies' strengths, rather than our own. Damage to physical property, however, is another matter. When done to harmful infrastructure such as weaponry, surveillance cameras, and 5G towers, it is not violence but a holy and righteous act.

Their symbols, monuments, flags, and temples, too, are ripe for attack. During the time of Elisha, Jehu summoned the priests of Baal to their own temple for a sacrifice then had his soldiers surround them and put every one to the sword. Then they "tore down the temple of Baal, and people have used it for a latrine to this day" (2 *Kings* 10:27). Thus, pissing and shitting on our enemies' symbols, including that badge of Molech falsely called 'the Star of David', is also a righteous act.

Speaking Truth to the medical-industrial complex.

Among the times I spoke Truth to Power was at a 'Listening Session on Public Health Emergencies Preparedness and Response Negotiations', conducted by the U.S. negotiating team to the World Health Organization (W.H.O.) on Apr. 11, 2024 and led by 'Ambassador' Pamela Hamamoto. I said the following…

To the Department of Health and Human Services and all you are taking orders from, to the World Health Organization, and to the various sycophants gathered here today to catch some crumbs from HHS' $2 trillion budget—

From Heaven, I unmask all of you, that you are unmasked on Earth, so that all shall know who you are and what you are and what you have done and whom you serve.

You are a Satanic, Molech-worshipping cult, serving deities of human sacrifice, murdering children in the womb, at the breast, and directly by the needle.

Who am I to say this? I am a man, and Man has authority over all the creations of men, meaning I have authority over all of you.

I am also exercising my authority in Christ to overcome all the power of the enemy. And you are the enemy: traitors to your country, traitors to Mankind.

You have exchanged the black robes of your secret societies with white coats and hospital scrubs, swapped sacrificial knives with poison needles, blood-drenched altars with hospital beds, and you have desecrated your public oaths with secret oaths.

Therefore, before the King of kings and Lord of lords, I decree all World Health Organization and United Nations talks shall collapse in dissension and disarray as you destroy each other.

So be it. So be it. And so be it.

Then, on Nov. 4, 2024, I sent Hamamoto the following email…

Hello Ms. Hamamoto —

You may recall me telling you that the WHO negotiations would fail. That is about to come to pass. The organization, and the one you represent, are destined for destruction, and I shall rejoice at their demise.

Meanwhile, we have observed your complicity in genocide as you play priestess to infernal deities. You too will meet unanswerable wrath in your coming appointment with Justice.

All this is decreed in Heaven and now effected on Earth.

Abdiel LeRoy

About a month later, I learned that she had resigned from her position.

Prayer Gets Results

I also attribute to intercession—that is to say, prayer spoken on behalf of others,...

- The release of Julian Assange.
- Thwarting escalation of War.
- Disrupting negotiations of the World Health Organization.
- Diverting hurricanes, and thwarting weather weapons.
- Exposing the Satanic paedophile and paedivore (child cannibalism) networks.

Another public serpent I went after was Dr. Peter Marks, former head of the FDA's Center for Biologics Evaluation and Research from 2016 to 2025. He was the U.S. government's main cheerleader of the 'vaccine' agenda and chief gatekeeper in silencing and gaslighting the injured and maimed. Marks even coined the name 'Operation Warp Speed', according to Dr. Paul Offit, a member of the FDA's advisory committee.

Marks is an exemplary psychopath—meaning someone who can kill without remorse—and makes even Anthony Fauci look like a schoolboy by comparison.

In a Feb. 13, 2025 interview with Victor Hugo Vaca Jr., I included in intercessory decree, "the downfall and destruction of Dr. Peter Marks, Pfizer's and Moderna's henchman at the FDA." I since learned that on Mar. 28, 2025, Marks was forced to resign.

Speaking truth to the sky.

But don't just take my word for it that prayer gets results. The following is from a Mar. 15, 2025 article by Victoria Bingham who was contending with heavy chemtrailing above her property. She reports,…

> "I pointed at the plane and said (out loud): 'I rebuke you in the name of Jesus Christ. This is God's property that you're messing with. He is maintaining my lot. The lines are fallen unto me in pleasant places. You have no business here. I rebuke you! You will be grounded and not fly again.'

"I was completely unprepared for what happened next. The plane was gone. The trails gone... Not a trail left behind... The trails should have been visible for hours. NOTHING. AFTER I PRAYED THE WHOLE THING FLAT OUT DISAPPEARED."

PROPHETIC FULFILMENTS AHEAD

... and in that day there shall be no more the Canaanite in the house of the Lord of hosts.

— ZECHARIAH 14:21

"Seize the prophets of Baal. Let none escape!" This was the command Elijah gave to the people after they saw him defeat his enemies in a contest on Mount Carmel (*1 Kings* 18). They took those false prophets down to the Kishon Valley and bashed their brains out until the once dry riverbed flowed with their blood.

This is one of my favourite Old-Testament episodes, and I dramatize it in my epic poem, *Elijah*. You may know the story. Elijah has King Ahab summon the prophets of Baal to Mount Carmel, then he announces a contest. They are to prepare an altar, sacrifice a bull on it, and call on their god to send down fire. Then he will prepare another altar, sacrifice another bull on it, and call on Yahweh to send down fire. "The god who sends down fire… is God!"

Baal's ministers go through the motions, calling on their god to no avail while Elijah mocks them. After they are exhausted, Elijah calls on the Most High who sends down fire of such vehemence that it burns up his offering and the entire altar with it. That's when the man of God issues his command, and the idolators are seized.

No need to present more evidence against them; they had already demonstrated their guilt by performing Satanic ritual, even cutting themselves with blades. No need for a verdict either, for the Almighty himself gave it when he sent down fire on Elijah's altar. All that remained was to carry out the prophet's sentence, and the crowd were more than willing to do it, delivering Sudden Adult Death Syndrome by mob violence.

Having heard testimony from survivors of Satanic atrocity, I no longer question why so much anger was unleashed against Baal's operatives that day. How many parents had lost their children to this cult? How many relatives had disappeared? How many had been extorted to fund the lavish lifestyles of this paedophile priesthood? How many were survivors themselves and carried a lifetime burden of trauma in their minds and bodies?

Nor do I question the order Jehu gave to his soldiers, a generation after Elijah, to surround the priests of Baal in their own temple after one of their rituals and put every one of them to the sword. Then the soldiers destroyed the temple and turned it into a shithouse (*2 Kings* 10:18-27).

After all the filth and corruption Ahab and Jezebel had inculcated with their infernal merger of state and cult religion, Jehu knew he had to clean house and, like Elijah, found a way to round up and isolate the cultists. He also made sure the righteous were not among them (v. 23) before unleashing retribution.

Each, in his own way and in his own badass style, effectively convened a Common-Law court. So too with Moses at the Red Sea. The men of Pharaoh's army were a distinct group who confirmed their guilt by their intention to slaughter civilians. The Almighty cordoned them off with pillars of fire and cloud then delivered sentence by closing the waters of the Red Sea over them. "Not one of them survived" (*Exodus* 14:28).

In all three judgments—against the prophets of Baal at Carmel, the priests of Baal in their temple, and the soldiers of Pharaoh at the Red Sea—the sentence was executed perfectly: not one innocent was punished; not one guilty was spared.

So it will be when Justice returns and the Seed War culminates with our spectacular victory over the serpent's spawn, as Jesus prophesied in the *Parable of the Wheat and the Tares* (or *Weeds*)....

> "... the good seed are the children of the kingdom, but the tares are the children of the wicked one. The enemy that sowed them is the devil; the harvest is the end of the world, and the reapers are the angels. As therefore the tares are gathered and burned in the fire, so shall it be in the end of this world. The Son of Man shall send

forth his angels, and they shall gather out of his kingdom all things that offend, and them which do iniquity, and cast them into a furnace of fire. There shall be wailing and gnashing of teeth. Then shall the righteous shine forth as the sun in the kingdom of their Father. Who hath ears to hear, let him hear."

— MATTHEW 13:38-43

First Enoch enriches the scene...

"And the exalted and those who hold the earth... shall be terrified, and they shall be downcast of countenance, and pain shall seize them, when they see that Son of Man sitting on the throne of glory... And he will deliver them to the angels for punishment, to execute vengeance on them because they have oppressed his children and his elect: They shall rejoice over them because the wrath of the Lord of Spirits resteth upon them, and his sword is drunk with their blood."

— FIRST ENOCH, 62:3-12

I put it to you, Brothers and Sisters, that studying *First Enoch* is a most profitable and worthy endeavour in these times, for it states right at the outset that its intended audience are "the elect and righteous who will be living in the day of tribulation, when all the wicked and godless are to be removed." As Rob Skiba points out, *First Enoch*, along with the books of *Jasher* and *Jubilees*, is one of the 'synchronized, Biblically-endorsed, extra-Biblical texts'. I have also found 2 *Baruch* and 2 *Esdras* to be sources of prophetic authority.

Not that I'm claiming expertise in end-times prophecy myself, though this menacing age compels me to study it more diligently. All those horns and horses, scrolls and seals and trumpets and what have you leave my head spinning. Yet I am confident that the Almighty will bring about great acts of spectacular and uncompromising Justice as he did through Elijah, Jehu, and Moses.

Among the other Scriptures that see us through is the whole of *Isaiah* 49. If you don't mind the plot spoiler, here are the closing two verses....

> ... *captives will be taken from warriors,*
> *and plunder retrieved from the fierce;*
> *I will contend with those who contend with you,*
> *and your children I will save.*
> *I will make your oppressors eat their own flesh;*
> *they will be drunk on their own blood, as with wine.*
> *Then all mankind will know*
> *that I, the Lord, am your Savior,*
> *your Redeemer, the Mighty One of Jacob.*
>
> — *ISAIAH* 49:25-26

This sounds like a Satanic blood ritual gone horribly wrong, a massive Freemason clusterfuck, and we will rejoice to see our would-be oppressors, deprived of their customary diet of children, turn on each other in a bloodbath of mutual and self-destruction. We will also see a sudden and massive downward transfer of wealth, as prophesied in *Job* 27....

> *Here is the fate God allots to the wicked,*
> *the heritage a ruthless man receives from the Almighty:...*
> *Though he heaps up silver like dust*
> *and clothes like piles of clay,*
> *what he lays up the righteous will wear,*
> *and the innocent will divide his silver.*
> *The house he builds is like a moth's cocoon,*
> *like a hut made by a watchman.*
> *He lies down wealthy, but will do so no more;*
> *when he opens his eyes, all is gone.*
>
> — JOB 27:13-19

The United Nations destroyed.

When it comes to the United Nations, I venture a prophecy more specific. The coming demise of that vipers' nest became obvious to me after it published an article titled *UN75: An Unexpected Message from the Future*. Contributed by Google's Chief Internet Evangelist, Vinton G. Cerf, it claims to channel a signal from the future in 2045, decoded by AI.

Conveniently for the organization's agenda, the message hails "digital cooperation," "sophisticated genetic modeling... to develop new species," and global cooperation to regulate "the pernicious and toxic consequences of unbridled social media." Translation: digital slavery, transhumanism, and censorship.

This echoes *1 Kings* 22. King Ahab asks his court prophets if he should go to war at Ramoth Gilead. Accustomed to telling the king what he wants to hear, they assure him he will be victorious, but one independent prophet, Micaiah, announces that a lying spirit was sent to the court prophets so that Ahab would go to war and get himself killed. Sure enough, during battle, a stray arrow goes between the sections of Ahab's armour, and by evening, he is dead.

Similarly, through witchcraft and divination, the United Nations is taking advice from a lying spirit cheerleading its war against Mankind and Creation, but as with Ahab, it shall suffer sudden and unexpected demise.

When We Are Judges

Will we participate in these feats of Judgment or just observe them? *First Enoch* also prophesies (95:3),…

> *Fear not the sinners, ye righteous,*
> *For the Lord will deliver them into your hands,*
> *That ye might execute judgment upon them*
> *According to your desires.*

I imagine, for example, being tasked with judging Dr. Peter Marks. The prosecution would play for the court an official FDA video, posted May 19, 2022, in which Marks states,...

> "Pregnant or breastfeeding women can certainly receive a COVID-19 vaccine... There is currently no evidence that any vaccines, including COVID-19 vaccines, cause fertility problems in either women or men."

Then the prosecution would put on screen excerpts from Pfizer's *Cumulative Analysis* document showing a spontaneous-abortion rate of more than 90% among pregnant women after they received the COVID injection. Next, they would prove that the FDA had this document in early May 2021, more than a year before Marks made his statement. Then, as judge, I would turn to Marks and say,...

> "Dr. Marks, you stand accused of the crime of genocide, and the evidence against you appears clear and compelling. If you acknowledge your guilt in this matter, you will receive a quick and merciful death this day. Or you can choose to proceed to Trial by Jury with presentation of witnesses and evidence. If the jury finds you guilty, then I cannot guarantee a merciful end. Among the sentences available to this jury is daily injections of COVID serums until your death, or hook-up to a ventilator machine, with or without sedation. Which course of action do you choose?"

As I said, Marks was the FDA's chief cheerleader for

'Operation Warp Speed' and even coined this title for the mass-injection campaign initiated by the first Trump administration, but he has received nowhere near the level of blame directed at his fellow conspirators in the medical-industrial complex such as Anthony Fauci or Rochelle Walensky. Also overlooked is Maggie Throup, the former U.K. vaccines minister. In a Dec. 4, 2021 press release, she wrote,...

> "The COVID-19 vaccines are safe and effective for pregnant women and I urge everyone to get their vaccines as soon as they can to secure this significant protection."

This was at least six months after regulators knew about the devastation COVID injections were causing, more likely a year after they knew. So I would put Throup through a similar process as Marks.

Swifter justice?

Yet Justice may proceed swifter than I have imagined if *Obadiah* 18 applies, a passage often cited by Dustin Nemos....

> *The house of Jacob will be a fire*
> *and the house of Joseph a flame;*
> *the house of Esau will be stubble,*
> *and they will set it on fire and consume it.*
> *There will be no survivors from the house of Esau.*

Here, the righteous line of Shem and Jacob unleash a breed-based purge against the seed of Satan and his rebellious angels, the seed of giants and monsters, those bloodlines that resumed after the Flood through Canaan, Cush, Nimrod, Esau, and the Edomites, that continued through the Pharisees, and are operating today through Freemasonry, secret societies, and death-cult 'Jews'.

Yet I caution my brothers and sisters against vengeance so indiscriminate that it sweeps up the innocent along with the guilty. Remember that Jesus warns us against pulling up the weeds that were sown with the wheat lest the wheat get pulled up too (*Matthew* 13:24-43).

Dreams and Visions

You're probably familiar with the prophet Joel's declaration…

> *And afterward,*
> *I will pour out my Spirit on all people.*
> *Your sons and daughters will prophesy,*
> *your old men will dream dreams,*
> *your young men will see visions.*
> *Even on my servants, both men and women,*
> *I will pour out my Spirit in those days.*
>
> — JOEL 2:28-29

Through some of the channels I follow, I hear a

swelling chorus of sons and daughters of the Most High prophesying in these days, having seen in their dreams everything from a zombie apocalypse to the new Jerusalem descending from Heaven.

Prophecy is given for our comfort, encouragement, and strength, as Paul tells us (*1 Corinthians* 14:3), but it can also be a form of warning in dreams. Thus, Joseph's Pharaoh was warned of a coming famine (*Genesis* 41), and stepfather Joseph was warned to take his wife and Jesus to Egypt (*Matthew* 2:13). These prophecies brought comfort, encouragement, and strength in the sense they enabled the recipients to avoid harm.

I try to remind myself of this after I've had a disturbing dream or outright nightmare. If it brings not comfort, encouragement, or strength, it may be a warning. I am also learning not to take every dream personally—thinking something bad is prophesied for me. Rather, I may be tasked with alerting sons and daughters of the Most High to what our enemies intend so that it may be foiled or avoided. I dare say some spectacular false-flag events planned by intelligence agencies—Mossad, CIA, MI6—have been cancelled because prophetic voices sounded the alarm in advance.

This is a form of spiritual espionage against them. You may recall that Elisha had such clear insight into the military ambushes Aram planned against Israel that the king of Aram thought there must be a spy in their midst. No, they tell him, "but Elisha, the prophet who is in Israel, tells the king of Israel the very words you speak in your bedroom" (*2 Kings* 6:12).

As the spiritual war heats up, the dreams and visions will come thick and fast. So too, of course, will fake prophets claiming, "God told me." Again, we may emulate the serpent, whose sensitive tongue probes the air, to discern whose tongue is forked. Another giveaway is "babbling like pagans" (*Matthew* 6:7) when false prophets and priests spew vain repetitions and empty words.

Therefore, as I add to the mix some of my own recent visions and dreams, and share with you what I think they mean (in *italics*), I won't be offended if you consult with the Holy Spirit, who is joined with your spirit (*John* 3:6; *Romans* 8:16; *1 Corinthians* 2:10-12, 6:17), to evaluate my interpretations.

Visions.

> A multitude of souls are lying on the surface of the Earth and looking out. They are all facing the same light. Some of the souls are in bliss, with joy and wonder on their faces, but then I see others whose faces are contorted with anguish and torment.

> *Upon our 'death', each of us faces the same light of the Most High, but the effect that light has on us produces opposites, bliss or torment, depending on the condition of our hearts. Some experience that light as Heaven, others as Hell. For some, facing the light of Love causes unbearable pain.*

I see before me a welcoming light through a thin veil of purple cloth.

The veil is 'death', and the light is the love that awaits me on the other side of it.

When in prayer for someone who repented of getting a COVID shot, I see in mind's eye that her mouth is open, her head tilted back, and Jesus is reaching in, grasping a serpent by its neck, and drawing the entire beast from her body, from her soul, and from every part of her being.

The COVID shots injected both physical and spiritual envenomation. The physical may be addressed through supplements and therapies, but the spiritual envenomation is addressed through repentance. If you are one who repents, I stand with you now before the throne of God, and present you for Jesus' healing and grace, wherein he removes the spiritual envenomation as extracting a snake. Then, having taken the serpent from you, he crushes its head and sends it to its appointed place, never to trouble you again. And so be it.

I see a heavenly host of angels awaiting orders and clamouring to be released so that they can come to the Earth and cleanse it of the Satanic scum now operating here. Jesus, their captain, has his hand raised. "Not yet, brothers. Let my sons and daughters show their mettle first."

We earnestly desire our Lord's return for we feel overwhelmed at times by the scale of evil and oppression plotted against us, and by the breadth and depth of Satan's operations that infest every human institution, but we are more than conquerors, equipped to "overcome all the power of the enemy," to take hold of the Kingdom of Heaven, and to tear down enemy strongholds with righteous fury. Now is the time to perform such warrior feats as will be written in Eternity.

I am sitting on a hillside, watching a line of silent souls walking across my line of sight from right to left. The line goes to a cliff edge where they quietly plunge to their deaths. Presiding over this is Satan, standing to the left of these souls at the cliff edge, and watching them. I watch Satan watching them.

This is a common meme. We are in disbelief at how cooperative so many have been in their own demise. We have tried calling out to them, tried warning them, tried standing in their way, but they don't listen, don't care. Facts don't matter. The only time they do rouse from sleepwalking is to attack us when we try to help them. On the very day I am writing this, I have seen video footage, from both Britain and the Netherlands, of people lining up for blocks to get a so-

called vaccine. We have reached the point of letting them get on with it now.

Dreams.

A woman comes against me with verbal attack. I rebuke her. She backs off with a sheepish smile. She tries again. This time, I unleash: "From Heaven, I decree your downfall and destruction that you are destroyed on Earth." Now, it turns into a male demon. Its eyes glaze over with white. I challenge it, "Look at me, demon!" But it cannot.

This confirms our authority to verbally strike our enemies and overcome them. We may even afflict them with blindness, as Elisha blinded the soldiers of Aram.

I run into an acquaintance on a train. She tells me, "The Sutton have decided they want to kill you." She tries to inject me with a hypodermic needle. I struggle with her and wake up.

Our enemies want to force lethal medication on us. The use of an acquaintance in this way suggests intense surveillance, betrayal, and possibly gang-stalking. Not sure what 'the Sutton' is. Satan, perhaps, or a secret society?

I am in an institution where one of the staff is closely observing me, looking for any excuse to declare me insane. I run out into a courtyard and scale a fence to escape.

Our enemies will target Christians with accusations of insanity to attempt psychological incarceration.

I am standing at a counter talking to an official. He has my passport open in front of him at the visa page. He seems to find a problem but I can barely hear what he's saying. I ask him to speak up. He repeats himself but no louder than before. I tell him I still can't hear him. Again, he repeats himself, but again, no louder than before. Something is handwritten in all-caps and black ink on one of the visa pages. It includes the phrase, "TAKEN BY FORCE!" in all-caps. The official is suggesting I wrote it. I know I didn't.

The slavemasters have stolen our birthright with ALL-CAPS on official documents, and they are making travel increasingly difficult. Will this lead to outright kidnapping at border crossings?

I am employed in a slaughterhouse. My job is to drag various livestock across the floor to an extermination machine that will butcher them. I am handed several ropes, each of which is inserted at the other end into the rectum of a living animal that is lying on the floor. I'm not sure if they are shocked or drugged. As I pull on the first set of ropes, I sob in sorrow for the animals. Then I am given a second set of ropes, and as I drag the second group of animals, I weep just as much as before.

Is another culling of human livestock planned? And why are these animals pulled by their rectums? This reminds me that the Chinese were doing fecal testing for 'COVID'.

I see a beautiful woman in a nightclub. She is talking to a man on a balcony. Two cavalcades of black cars, operated by rival gangs, converge on the street below. I think they are coming to fight over the girl but instead, they go into a hospital and start doing summary executions of hospital staff. I see black gangsters shooting black employees in the head. Some of the staff are lined up against a wall. A white female nurse is being questioned if she is a Christian. She fears for her life and doesn't know how to answer. She says, "Lots of people are Christians."

So vile are the COVID crimes that even rival gangs will unite to take revenge on the medical murderers.

I am taking part in some kind of banking exercise that involves us handing in our gold and silver for safe keeping in return for paper receipts. I feel great anxiety, not knowing if I will ever get it back.

Banks and governments want to keep your precious metals and give you worthless paper receipts for them. It is outright theft. They will never honour those receipts, and you will never get your metals back. So do not register, declare, or deposit gold or silver with them. They want to steal it (and it wouldn't be the first time).

I am playing a piano concerto with an orchestra behind me, but doing so on a computer keyboard instead of a piano. The keys play notes instead of letters.

My writing is a symphony. (Permit me an occasional boast.)

INTERCESSORY DECREES

I close out this series with three intercessory decrees that encapsulate most of my prior discourse. If thou wilt add thine 'Agreed' or 'So be it', it shall be done for us by our Father in Heaven...

INTERCESSORY DECREE 1
PROTECTING CHILDREN, UNMASKING AND DEMOLISHING THE SYNAGOGUE OF SATAN

We stand now before the throne of the Most High, clothed in the righteousness of Christ, knowing that our prayers are powerful and effective, that whatsoever we bind on Earth in bound in Heaven, whatsoever we loose on Earth is loosed in Heaven, knowing we have authority to overcome all the power of the enemy, that when two or more of us agree about anything, it shall be done for us by our Father in Heaven, that what the righteous decree, the Holy One carries out. Therefore, in this authority,...

Protection.

From Heaven, we turn all directed energy weapons back on their creators and deployers that they are burned to a crisp on Earth. "If I'm a man of God, let fire descend from Heaven and consume thee and thy men!" From Heaven, we destroy all their 'Silent Weapons for Quiet

Wars' that they are destroyed on Earth. From Heaven, we close the portals that have given demons access to Earth, and from Heaven, we strip the disguise from all demonic entities and deny them a hiding place, so that all shall know who they are and what they are and what they have done and whom they serve.

Children.

From Heaven, we expose the atrocities enacted against children—including cannibalism, drugging, hunting, imprisonment, kidnapping, live organ-harvesting, mind-control, murder, mutilation, ritual sacrifice, slavery, and torture—and the perpetrators of those atrocities, that they are exposed on Earth, and we decree that no chamber, dungeon, or tunnel is deep enough or dark enough to hide their crimes.

From Heaven, we flood the venues of atrocity with a bright, unanswerable light from which none can hide, and from Heaven, we command the very walls of those venues, including the walls of Carnarvon Castle in Wales, and the very trees of groves, to tell the horrors they have seen and to expose the perpetrators.

From Heaven, we shut down the supply of adrenochrome that it is shut down on Earth, so that all who would take it are henceforth parched and starved.

And we declare over the boys and girls now held in captivity or targeted for sacrifice, "Do not touch my anointed ones, do my prophets no harm!" From Heaven, we release them from captivity that they are released on

Earth. And we decree upon all who bear the seal of the Holy Spirit, "Do not touch my anointed ones, do my prophets no harm!"

Unmasking.

From Heaven, we unmask Donald Trump and his Satanic network that they are unmasked on Earth, and from Heaven, we overturn his agendas of destruction, including destruction by surveillance, by AI, and by so-called vaccines, that they are all overturned on Earth.

From Heaven, we unmask all Controlled-Opposition operatives, that they are unmasked on Earth, and from Heaven, we strip the fleece from the wolves in sheep's clothing that they are stripped on Earth.

Demolishing the Synagogue of Satan.

From Heaven, we expose and destroy the government, state, and military that calls itself 'Israel', that it is exposed and destroyed on Earth. From Heaven, we set the people of Palestine free from their oppressors that they are set free on Earth. From Heaven, we decree the downfall and destruction of the House of Rothschild that it is destroyed on Earth, as surely as the House of Ahab was destroyed, by which the head of every son was cut off and gathered in baskets.

From Heaven, we deny breeding to all Satanic bloodlines on Earth and to the Synagogue of Satan and to the 'Jewish State' of Fake Israel. From Heaven, we destroy their penises with impotence and disease so that their filthy seed shall no more spread, and from Heaven we make barren their filthy wombs.

And from Heaven, we unleash upon secret-society members at every level, from so-called initiate to so-called adept, confusion, fear, and dread. And we decree upon secret-society members at every level, "you will henceforth and immediately turn on each other and destroy each other, even eating each other's flesh and drinking each other's blood."

From Heaven, we decree the downfall and destruction of Dr. Peter Marks, Pfizer's and Moderna's henchman at the FDA, who orchestrated the murder of infants in the womb and infants at the breast; and the downfall and destruction of Maggie Throup, former U.K. vaccines minister, also complicit in the sacrifice of little ones to Molech.

All this is decreed in Heaven and now effected on Earth. So be it, so be it, and so be it!

Download additional copies at https://Geni.us/Decree1.

INTERCESSORY DECREE 2
ON BANKING, CENSORSHIP, AND SURVEILLANCE

We stand now before the throne of the Most High, clothed in the righteousness of Christ, knowing that our prayers are powerful and effective, that whatsoever we bind on Earth is bound in Heaven, whatsoever we loose on Earth is loosed in Heaven, that we have authority to overcome all the power of the enemy, and that when two or more of us agree about anything, it shall be done for us by our Father in Heaven, and that what the righteous decree, the Holy One carries out. And we remember that in Heaven, there is no thief to break in or steal.

Therefore, in this authority,...

Banking.

From Heaven, we break the chains of taxation, inflation, confiscation, and debt that they are broken on Earth, from Heaven we bind all financial attack against us that it is bound on Earth, and from Heaven, we restore all that has been stolen from us.

From Heaven, we release funds to the righteous that they receive them on Earth. We declare over our lives, as was declared for Joseph, "The Lord gave him success in everything he did." And from Heaven we restore our Birthright, we who are made in the image of the Most High and whose hearts are one with the Son of Man, that our Birthright is restored on Earth.

From Heaven, we break the locks on the vaults and treasuries of the banker tyrants that they are broken on Earth; from Heaven we loose their funds and property—their gold, silver, land, mansions, cars, yachts, and wine collections—that they are loosed on Earth and given to the righteous; and from Heaven, we decree the downfall and destruction of Agustín Carstens, the human toad heading the Bank of International Settlements. We plunder you, central bankers and your accomplices, that you are plundered on Earth, as surely as the true Israelites plundered the Egyptians.

Censorship.

From Heaven, we overthrow the censorship perpetrated against us that it is overthrown on Earth, from Heaven, we bind, blind, and mute the censors that they are bound, blinded, and muted on Earth, and put to everlasting shame. Then from Heaven, we restore the income denied to us by all forms of censorship and restriction that it is restored on Earth.

Surveillance.

From Heaven, we blind the tyrants and their surveillance so that they are blinded on Earth. From Heaven, we unmask them so that they are unmasked on Earth, so that all shall know who they are and what they are and what they have done and whom they serve. And from Heaven, we reveal even the whispers and secrets of their own bedchambers.

All this is decreed in Heaven and now effected on Earth. So be it. So be it. And so be it!

Download additional copies at https://Geni.us/Decree2.

INTERCESSORY DECREE 3
ON WAR

So the tyrants want war. Is to protect us, the domestic populations? Or is it to destroy us? I have no quarrel with the Russian people, nor with the Chinese, nor with the people of Iran. They live and love and breathe as we live and love and breathe.

Is war to protect us? Or is to drive even more profits into the military-industrial complex while driving the people into deeper and deeper poverty?

As Orwell said, the purpose of war is to blow to pieces the labours of the people as bombs are blown to pieces.

I do not consent! Brothers and Sisters, say it with me... I do not consent!

You generals and admirals and air marshals, captains and lieutenants and wing commanders, men and women of every rank, say it with me, I DO NOT CONSENT! And oh yes, you wing commanders, doing nothing while the people of your nation are sprayed with poisons. How brave!

Where is the informed consent for your wars, you tyrants? I did not agree to be impoverished or make one sacrifice to serve your geopolitical ends, you parasites, you snakes, you brood of vipers.

We know your schemes. You attack the domestic population and call it the enemy's work with your false-flag events, as Orwell told us you would. You will try it again to stir up patriotic fervour for war. Well, we're not buying it!

You servants of the Father of Lies, we overthrow you in Heaven that you are overthrown on Earth. We destroy your weapons in Heaven that they are destroyed on Earth, and we disband your mercenary forces, that they are disbanded on Earth. And we silence in Heaven, that they are silenced on Earth, the liars and propagandists who call for war.

We destroy all you destroyers, that you are destroyed on Earth. You are destroyed as surely as the chariots of Pharaoh were destroyed. This is prophesied. This is decreed!

Go then to your appointed places, you merchants of violence, to where there is never a moment's joy, and there you shall find all the war and destruction you ever wished to inflict on others. This is the name of Jesus, Yeshua, the Son of Man.

So be it, so be it, and so be it!

Download additional copies at https://Geni.us/Decree3.

INTERCESSORY DECREE 4
COMPLETION OF DELIVERANCE

I heard a preacher talking about curses. Among their effects, he listed: repeated or chronic illnesses, especially where doctors cannot find any normal cause; family alienation; and financial insufficiency. He said,…

> "A curse is like a long evil arm from the past, and you don't know how far back… and every time you're just about to succeed or get to where you want to be, this evil arm trips you up, and you have to get up and start again, and you get so far, and you're tripped up again, and that really becomes the story of your life… A dark shadow from the past over your life, shutting out the sunlight of God's blessing, and you can see other people walking in the sunlight, and you know it's there and real, but somehow the sun very seldom seems to shine fully on you."

I struggle with this on a logical basis because…

1. Jesus became a curse for us (*Galatians* 3:13), thereby annulling all curses against us.

2. Jesus cancelled all legal code that stood opposed to us, nailing it to the Cross (*Colossians* 2:14), so any legal agreements made by our ancestors are null and void. He has also wiped out any evidence against us.

3. A curse undeserved does not come to rest (*Proverbs* 26:2) and, when one is in Jesus Christ, clothed with his righteousness, no curse *is* deserved.

So what am I missing here? Are these scriptures like keys wherein it's our job to turn those keys? Has the deliverance happened at the level of our spirit, which is joined with the Holy Spirit (*1 Corinthians* 6:17), but then needs to be be processed through the soul?

In other words, having been made whole at the core level, as marrow in the bones, do we need to foster the expression of that wholeness from the inside out, going from the marrow to the bones themselves, and from the bones through the whole body?

To that end, I have written the following *Intercession of Completed Deliverance* and invite you to join me in saying it, then to add your "Agreed" or "So be it" in the comments, so that the completion of deliverance shall proceed in your life and body and in mine…

We stand now before the Throne of the Most High, clothed in the righteousness of Jesus Christ who died to set us free from every curse, who overcame death, who ascended, and whose resurrection power is ours, he who is at the right hand of the Holy One and even now intercedes for us as one speaks for a friend.

We approach this Throne with confidence, knowing our prayers are powerful and effective, that whatsoever we bind on Earth is bound in Heaven, whatsoever we loose on Earth is loosed in Heaven, that we have authority to overcome *all* the power of the enemy, and that what the righteous decree, the Holy One carries out.

And in this authority, we banish from our life and existence, that they are banished on Earth, the ancient curse against Adam that said, "In the sweat of thy face shalt thou eat bread" (*Genesis* 3:19), and the ancient curse Cain deserved that said, "a fugitive and a vagabond shalt thou be in the Earth" (*Genesis* 4:12).

From Heaven, we bind and destroy all curses against us and all ties that have damaged or delayed us, diluted or dissipated our efforts, harmed, hindered, sabotaged, sickened, or stolen from us, that they are bound and destroyed on Earth, as surely as Moses destroyed the Golden Calf of idolatry and crushed it to powder as fine as dust.

> "I took that sinful thing of yours, the calf you had made, and burned it in the fire. Then I crushed it and ground it

to powder as fine as dust and threw the dust into a stream that flowed down the mountain" (Deuteronomy 9:21).

In Heaven, we shine the irresistible light of Jesus Christ on the origin of every curse, revealing the who, the what, the when, and the where. We uproot them permanently and send them to their appointed place, never to trouble us again.

And from Heaven, we bind, blind, and mute the originators, perpetrators, and conspirators of curses and ties against us, that they are bound, blinded, and muted on Earth.

Before the throne of Yahweh, our Creator, we annul the contract with our father in which he ...., and the contract with our mother in which she ....

In Heaven, we claim and confirm that nothing can separate us from the Love of God, by which present, past, and future are healed. In Heaven, we decree completion of Jesus' victory and resurrection power in our lives.

In Heaven, we confirm that all legal code and all evidence against us are wiped out. Our old filthy garments have been removed, and we now stand anew in holy raiment, clothed in the very righteousness of Christ, and if Satan dare to speak, we remind the Court that any accuser seeking to cast the first stone must first be without sin himself. Thus is Satan self-condemned while we are found innocent and holy in the eyes of the Most High. It is finished, and the case against us is dismissed... eternally.

We are overcomers, by definition, and even now overcome the physical afflictions we have experienced or are now experiencing. From Heaven, we bestow upon our lives and bodies healing, restoration, rejuvenation, and forgiveness of sins.

> "Son, be of good cheer; thy sins be forgiven thee... Arise, take up thy bed, and go unto thine house."
>
> — MATTHEW 9:2,6

In Heaven, we bestow protection from every evil attack, wherein no weapon forged against us will prevail —financial, physical, psychological, or any other. From Heaven, we restore to our life everything that was stolen from us, including our innocence.

All this is decreed in Heaven and now effected on Earth.

So be it. Agreed. And hallelujah.

CONCLUSION

There's no Great Awakening.
Just lemmings hitting snooze on the apocalypse, drooling
  through the end times like braindead zombies.
And when you try to shake them awake?
They bite.

— SIR ESCANOR, NOTE ON SUBSTACK,
OCT. 6, 2025

I conclude this book with a deep sense of failure. The very frequency with which people *still* call legislation 'law', including people who purport to stand for Truth and Freedom and should know better, indicts my efforts. All my writings, books, articles, and carefully crafted comments on social media seem to have had zero impact in deprogramming this idolatry.

As I write this, there is a balcony to my left. Were I to

jump from it, I would fall and probably suffer injury. On the way down, my body would accelerate at roughly 10 metres per second per second. This is a physical law, and much as I might like to take enormous bounds over the jungle canopy, I don't have the authority to change the constant acting on my body. For…

ONLY GOD CAN MAKE LAW!

Yet almost everyone who talks about Truth and Freedom makes the fundamental error, and possibly fatal error, of calling the legislation of men and women 'law'. I expect it of tyrants, of course, blind to their own blindness and deceitful to the core, but not of those who purport to oppose them, much less of Christians who have the Mind of Christ.

Calling legislation 'law' is supporting false authority, it is slavery of the mind, and if the mind is not free, how shall the body and the rest of our lives be free? We're not talking quaint semantics here; this is a matter of Life and Death.

So if there is one idea or course of action you take away from this book, let it be that henceforth you never call legislation 'law', much less the regulations and executive orders of creatures who devour children by night and sweat out tyrant texts by day. You have authority over them, and so do I. Also, correct those around you who idolize the work of demons by calling it, 'law'.

Another failure I own is that, in the prior *Battle*

Manuals for Freedom trilogy, I quoted several people who, I later found out or came to suspect, are Controlled Opposition, that is to say, 'white tiles' on the Freemason floor. They include: Mike Adams, Miki Klan, Lara Logan, Peter McCullough, Ann Vandersteel, and Bret Weinstein. As for Robert F. Kennedy Jr., he is perhaps the most despicable all, traitor even to his former self or rather, to the character he used to play.

I considered revising the entire collection to remove or paraphrase their contributions, but the effort is not justified. Even villains are capable of speaking truths and are quotable when they do.

One correction I *did* make was to remove my misguided welcome of a 'Great Awakening' as antidote to the 'Great Reset' planned by the likes of Klaus Schwab. No, the 'Great Awakening' is another white tile on the Freemason floor. As Sir Escanor warns in a Substack post of Oct. 7, 2025,…

> "Understand the operating system. Secret societies and mystery schools aren't united by doctrine, they're united by outcome. The glue is conflict. They manufacture opposites, feed both sides, and collect the winnings. Duality—left foot, right foot, marching in the same direction, building the same throne, through conflict! This isn't nihilism, it's clarity. You can't build solutions while mistaking the cage for a chapel, or the beast's priests for allies."

So I have put away that childish thing of embracing a

'Great Awakening'. Rather, I herald a 'Great Reckoning' when, like a mighty river, Justice returns.

I question too my former praises for the 'Law of the Land', which stands in opposition to the Maritime, or Admiralty, corporate code orchestrated to steal from us. If it means Common Law, with its basic principle of "Do no harm," then it is worthy of praise for it accords with Jesus' command to love others as we love ourselves, but I caution against following fake heroes who pretend to champion it. Bear in mind that in *Revelation*, after the First Beast has arisen from the Sea, the Second Beast arises from the Earth, not to oppose the First Beast but to work with it (13:11-15). Beware of labels meant to seduce us and placate us, and beware of phoney saviours riding a white horse or, worse, the pale green horse of Death (*Revelation* 6:1-8).

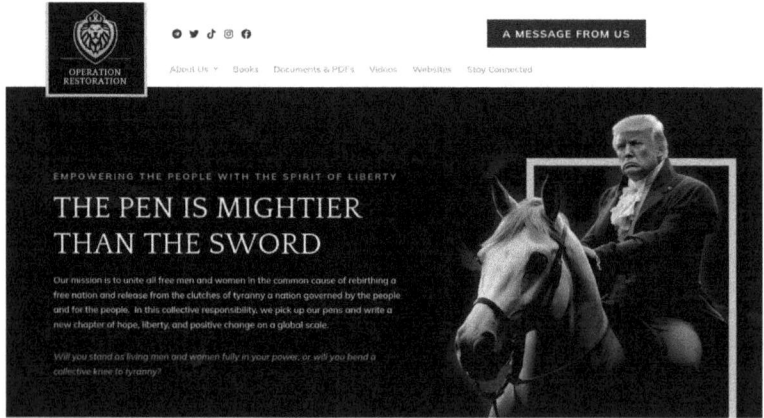

Deception runs deep, but by Grace we shall see

through it. Even if it hides behind a smokescreen, the smoke will clear in time.

As for "naming the Jew," I find it more helpful and unambiguous to name Satan's spawn and servants according to their shibboleths (*Judges* 12:4-6), starting with dual citizenship with 'Israel', sure sign of an infiltrator. Another, of course, is the secret oath. Those awfully cooperative Freemasons and other secret-society filth have done the job of lumping themselves together into a culpable cult by this abomination alone. You cannot serve two masters, it's as simple as that. Anyone who has sworn a secret oath has declared war on Jesus.

Now, Brothers and Sisters, I invite you to join me in the Further Exploration section where I expand on the themes we've looked at thus far. Throughout this *Battle Manuals for Freedom* series, I have diligently sought to write what is upright and true (*Ecclesiastes* 12:10), and ask that you accept the will for the deed in accordance with the Grace that is yours and mine.

Much love,
Abdiel LeRoy, 2025

FURTHER EXPLORATION

Following are some recent selections from my *Verses Versus Empire Collection* (https://Geni.us/Potus) in four parts...

1. Waging Spiritual War

2. Insights for Christians

3. Exposing Crisis Actors and Psychological Operations

4. Short Fiction

PART I
WAGING SPIRITUAL WAR

LOVE MY ENEMIES? YOU GOTTA BE KIDDING!

"Love your enemies."

How does that work nowadays when your enemies are perpetrating genocide, harvesting children, and trying to ruin this planet for generations to come? You want me to love a Satanic cult who swear secret oaths to secret societies, serve Molech and Baal, and devote their lives to relentless and remorseless harm against others?

This supposed command comes from *Matthew* 5, the same passage in which Jesus calls on us to pluck out our own eye, or cut off our own hand, if either offend us, and to give our coat to he who would take our shirt.

Why would Jesus place these impossible burdens on us when, elsewhere, he states that the only requirements are to love the Lord your God with all your heart and mind, and to love others as ourselves? Why, when righteousness is conferred on us by faith alone, would

Jesus spoil this perfect grace by bolting on extra commands?

Could his intention be to convince us instead that it is futile and absurd to seek righteousness by fulfilling commands, in much the same way he gave the rich young man an Eleventh Commandment to follow, after the man claimed he had kept the previous Ten (*Mark* 10:17-21)?

If that's the type of righteousness you seek, then here are some more commands in the vein of *Matthew* 5... If they take your income, let them take your property too. If they defile your body, let them defile your children's bodies too. And if they put a swab up your nose, let them stick a needle in your arm too!

But why stop there? If they rape your wife, let them rape your daughter too. If they steal your car, let them have your truck as well. Or if they kill your dog, let them kill your cat too.

Why would Jesus put loving one's enemies in the same category as self-mutilation if not to drive home the absurdity of commandment-keeping when, instead, righteousness comes from faith alone?

I'll tell you what loving my enemies means to me. It means I strike them, so help me God, with all the love that Jesus grants me. It means I love them as Jesus loved the moneychangers when he whipped them out of the temple or when he called the Pharisees a brood of vipers condemned to Hell. It means I love as my namesake, the seraph Abdiel, loved in John Milton's *Paradise Lost*, when he struck Satan with such force that Satan fell to his knees. "Zeal for my father's house consumes me," sayeth the Lord. Well, zeal for my father's house consumes me too.

Love my enemies? I'm going to love them alright. I'm going to love them to death.

December 2023

CHRISTIANS SHOULD BE CURSING COPS
THE EXERCISE OF BOTH LOGICAL AND SPIRITUAL AUTHORITY WHEN TYRANTS RULE

I am watching a presentation by Larken Rose titled "*It Can't Happen Here!*", and it's got me thinking. In it, he quotes from the Constitution of the U.S.S.R, "Citizens of the USSR are guaranteed freedom of speech, of the press and of assembly, meetings, street processions and demonstrations." And from the Constitution of the People's Republic of China, "Citizens of the People's Republic of China enjoy freedom of speech, of the press, of assembly, of association, of procession and of demonstration."

I also recently found, in the Costa Rican constitution, "La propiedad es inviolable," meaning, property is inviolable or that, property is sacred, even as uniformed Costa Rican thugs were demolishing homes and businesses on orders from the corrupt local mayor.

For every nation gives lip service to Rights, and even governments that obviously practice Satanic arts are technically signed up to some virtue-signalling code of behaviour such as a constitution or a charter. This underscores the apostle Paul's observation that Satan masquerades as an angel of light and that his servants masquerade as servants of righteousness (*2 Corinthians* 11:14-15).

Meanwhile, among the rank and file population, we see Paul's equation play out in self-righteous compliance with official absurdities, to the extent that they will denounce, and even betray, those who stand up for their Rights.

So here's what we do when dealing with Rights-desecrating enforcers, including cops, bureaucrats, and judges. Tell them they are breaking the Law—whether you define that Law in terms of safeguarding inherent Rights or you invoke some language in a constitution, bill of rights, international declaration, court precedent, legislation, or what have you—and that, as stated in *Deuteronomy* 27:26, he who breaks the law is UNDER A CURSE!

> "Meaning that, from this day forward, you will not have a moment's joy for the rest of your life and, in the life to come, you will have eternal torment. Would you like to rethink your position today?"

Then you may wish to inflict further consequences on these agents of extortion, enslavement, and execution…

"You will not sleep though your bed is soft, you will not eat though your plate is full, you will go to your torment, despised of God and Mankind, never to trouble me or anyone else ever again."

Am I saying a constitution is 'law'? Hell, no! Nor is anything else written or decreed by Man. Men and women are not capable of writing anything that even touches the realm of Law. That is the Creator's remit alone though, to my great disappointment with Humanity in general and with dissidents in particular, almost everyone continues to call legislation and regulations and court precedents 'law' (and currency 'money').

But constitutions *are* Law to those who swear an oath to them, for they are contractually bound to their promise.

Remember your Authority too. As stated in the documentary *Strawman*, "Government is a creation of Man, and a creation of Man can never be above Man." Same goes for other creations of men such police and military, courts and corporations, bureaucracies and banks. This is the Authority of Logic alone. Cops who think they can issue "lawful orders" to us are deluded. No, we issue lawful orders to *them*, and if they disobey, we are entitled to arrest *them*!

Yet I do not rest on the Authority of Logic alone when I have the infinitely more powerful, and unanswerable, Authority of the Son of Man—whom some call Jesus and some call Yeshua—to "overcome all the power of the enemy." He exhorts us to wield devastating spiritual violence against our enemies as we enforce and expand the Kingdom of Heaven on Earth (*Matthew* 11:12). Thus, when I invoke the above Scripture from *Deuteronomy*, I am invoking the power of Jesus' curse against the unfruitful fig tree, by which it was withered the very next day (*Mark* 11:12-14,19-21).

I remember too our great exemplars from the Old Testament, especially Elijah who by words alone slaughtered multitudes of false prophets, false priests, and men at arms, along with the entire royal household of Israel. Therefore, along with the declarations I have given you above, I have in my weaponry,…

> "From Heaven, I decree your downfall and destruction that you are destroyed on Earth, never to trouble me or Mankind ever again."

Though I have begun to wield these weapons, I can't say they're fully battle-tested yet, but they are fashioned from deep study and tempered in an armourer's forge afire with vexing encounters I and others have had with uniformed organisms. Brothers and Sisters, we have everything we need to be "more than conquerors" (*Romans* 8:37). We can quote our enemies' constitutions as Law to them, and trigger an avalanche of curses upon them for violating them.

Though the so-called 'Truth Movement' or the so-called 'Freedom Movement' widely acknowledge that we are in a 'spiritual war', they seem to reduce it to an information war about what the truth is and who is telling it. That's one element but the more critical battle is against the virtue-signalling and, when it suits them, truth-telling puppet masters and their front-line agents of extortion, enslavement, and extermination. It is here that we Christians will prove most decisive and destructive to the Satanic agenda.

Ultimately, my calls to action are no more and no less than wielding our inherent authorities, both of Logic and of spiritual violence; they are no more and no less than taking Jesus at his word. So I suggest we put these weapons to powerful and immediate use.

September 2025

A COVID AMNESTY IS EVIL AND UNGODLY

The COVID tyrants, and their media servants, seem to be pinning their hopes on the idea that Christians forgive, no matter what. They seem to think we will pardon their crimes with neither repercussion nor reproach and leave them at large to go about their next round of Satanic business.

It doesn't work like that. It never did. And we have a blueprint of exemplary forgiveness from Joseph in the Old Testament. It goes like this (excerpted from my book series, *The Gourmet Gospel*):

Joseph's brothers threatened his life and sold him into slavery at the age of 17 (*Genesis* 37:18-28). More than 20 years later, when he is Pharaoh's right-hand man in Egypt, those brothers appear before him on the verge of destitution (*Genesis* 42). He recognizes them, but they do not know who he is.

What example does Joseph give us here? Does he

immediately declare himself to them, embrace them, and throw open the granaries of Egypt to his former tormentors? No. He continues to conceal his identity while putting them through a series of tests to see if their hearts have changed.

The first evidence of this is when he overhears them saying, "Surely we are being punished because of our brother. We saw how distressed he was when he pleaded with us for his life, but we would not listen. That's why this distress has come upon us." This moves Joseph to tears, though he weeps them in secret.

Forgiveness has begun, but it is not yet complete. More tests follow, as Joseph sends his brothers back to Canaan to fetch the youngest, Benjamin, while keeping another, Simeon, hostage. When they return, and Joseph sees Benjamin, his only full brother among the group (the rest being half-brothers), he again weeps in secret.

Final proof of his brothers' repentance, however, comes after Joseph has Benjamin framed for the theft of a silver cup, as the group set out for Canaan a second time. The penalty for Benjamin is to become an Egyptian slave. At this point, the ten other brothers could simply have abandoned the youngest to bondage in Egypt, as they had done with Joseph all those years ago, but instead go back to face the music together.

Finally, when Judah offers to pay the penalty of slavery himself by taking Benjamin's place, Joseph is overcome and can no longer conceal his identity. He sees the repentance of his brothers, their readiness to take upon themselves the suffering they had once inflicted, and declares himself to them. Now bursts his mighty heart; forgiveness is complete.

In this example, forgiveness goes hand in hand with the repentance of the offender; the wronged and the wronger cooperate. The crime is not overlooked, whitewashed, or generalized, not diminished, downplayed, or diluted. Joseph says to his brothers, "I am your brother, Joseph, the one you sold into Egypt... You intended to harm me, but God intended it for good."

Joseph's story also demonstrates that forgiveness is not just a religious concept but a human capacity, built into our nature, and once bestowed inwardly, can find its outer expression. Had Joseph been too hasty in his forgiveness, he would not only have robbed his own heart of its time and process, but denied his brothers the gift of repentance.

Yet most Christians put the cart of outward forgiveness before the horse of inward forgiveness. And how many would dare do so "unchristian" a thing as frame his own brother for a theft? What emerges from Joseph's story is a skilfully choreographed dance of forgiveness, a poetic drama written by the Holy Spirit in human hearts.

So too, in Shakespeare's *The Tempest*. At the start of the play, Prospero relates to his daughter Miranda that he had been Duke of Milan until his own brother, Antonio, usurped the kingdom, betrayed it to the king of Naples, and set the two of them adrift in a condemned vessel to die.

But they survived, and Prospero, using his magical

powers, assisted by the spirit Ariel, imprisons his would-be murderers and confronts them with their crimes. Only when he is satisfied they are "full of sorrow and dismay" does he conclude, "The rarer action is/ In virtue than in vengeance. They being penitent,/ ... Go release them, Ariel" (V.i.27-30).

In both cases, the two maltreated men bring their tormentors within their own power and discover the repentant condition of their hearts before forgiveness is bestowed.

Therefore, when the unrepentant tormentors of our race come to us today demanding we wipe from remembrance their crimes against humanity so they may have a blank cheque to commit fresh atrocity, they only multiply their culpability. Rather, let us heed the commands given us in *Revelation* concerning Babylon, giving back to them as they have given, paying back double for what they have done, and giving them as much torture and grief as they doled out to our kin (18:4-7). Amnesty be damned!

November 2023

WHEN A TYRANT BEGS YOU FOR MERCY

Imagine the COVID tyrant you despise the most sitting before you. By Heaven's decree, you are there to deliver verdict and judgment about what should happen to them. Today, your word is law to the tyrant…

This is not idle fantasy, this will come to pass. The *Book of Enoch*, which belongs in the Bible even though most Bibles exclude it, states, "Fear not the sinners, ye righteous;/ For again will the Lord deliver them into your hands,/ That ye may execute judgment upon them according to your desires." (*Enoch* 95.3)

Also, according to the *Book of Jubilees*, Cain, who committed the first murder, was killed when his house fell on him. "With a stone he had killed Abel, and by a stone he was killed in righteous judgment./ For this reason, it was ordained on the heavenly tablets, with the instrument with which a man kills his neighbour, with the same shall he be killed. In the same manner that he wounded him, in like manner shall they deal with him." (*Jubilees* 4:32-33).

So, bearing in mind that Cain was killed by his own murder weapon, what judgment will you execute upon your chosen tyrant? I'll go first...

Maggie Throup was the 'vaccines minister' in Britain from September 2021 to September 2022. On Dec. 4, 2021, she said in a press release, "The COVID-19 vaccines are safe and effective for pregnant women and I urge everyone to get their vaccines as soon as they can to secure this significant protection."

This was more than six months after Pfizer sent regulators its *Cumulative Analysis* document showing that, out of 28 potential babies of injected mothers, 26 died by spontaneous abortion, and there was one neonatal death. Only one had a normal outcome (p.12).

But then Maggie Throup told pregnant women in Britain COVID-19 'vaccines' were safe and effective. I've got the documents, I've got the evidence.

So this is what I will say to Maggie Throup, "You have a choice. We are quite willing to give you due process. You can come before our Common-Law court, hear the charges against you, hear evidence against you, hear the witnesses against you, and have a representative in your defence. The verdict will be declared and, if you are found guilty, sentence will be delivered. Among the sentences at the disposal of this court is death by COVID injection.

"Or, if you decide you don't want to go through a court hearing, you can opt for a quick death today, carried out as painlessly as possible."

That's what I would tell her. And I expect many of the tyrants would opt for the merciful end of a quick death, knowing that the evidence against them is irrefutable, rather than hear the witnesses against them.

So what will *you* say when one of them appears before *you* for judgment?

April 2024

YE SHALL DESTROY THE FREEMASONS

"Almost any sect, cult, or religion will legislate its creed into law if it acquires the political power to do so."

— ROBERT A. HEINLEIN

Let's do a brief exercise in Logic. It begins with observing that, since 2020, medical tyranny has been rolled out throughout the world using the same measures, the same governmental decrees, and the same bioweapons, and all at the same time. We were not privy to all the communications that orchestrated this, but we saw the outcome.

With me so far? Now, secret coordination means a secret organization is at work—that is to say, a secret society—and as you may have heard, secret-society members swear secret oaths. Swearing a secret oath nullifies any public oath, whether to Constitution, Oath of Office, Constable's Oath, Hippocratic Oath, religious vow, and even marriage vows. Given all we have seen these past few years, we can be in no doubt the secret oath has supplanted the public oath at every turn.

As Christ reminds us, you cannot serve two masters (*Matthew* 6:24). He will spit out of his mouth those who are neither hot or cold for him (*Revelation* 3:16), he will defleece the wolves in sheep's clothing, and at the Judgment, he will order out of his presence virtue-signalling claimants to Salvation (*Matthew* 7:21-23).

Secret societies also perform secret rituals, and I have heard enough courageous testimony from their victims by now, all reporting the same kinds of horrors perpetrated at every level of society and in every nation, to know these rituals involve atrocity and torture and that they sear the conscience of any initiate.

This explains why doctors and nurses, princes and presidents and prime ministers, police and courts, along with many more operatives of state, crown, and corporation, can and do kill without remorse—the very definition of a psychopath. It also explains why hospital beds have become sacrificial altars, and hospital wards torture chambers, why injections now do the work of sacrificial knives and white coats the work of black robes.

Yet, even without our brave witnesses, the bloodthirsty Freemason oaths are atrocity enough to seal their destruction. At the First-Degree level, according to evangelicaltruth.com, the initiate swears to secrecy "under no less a penalty than that of having my throat cut across, my tongue torn out by its roots, and buried in the rough sands of the sea at low-water mark…"

At the Second Degree, the penalty is "having my left breast torn open, my heart plucked out, and given as a prey to the wild beasts of the field and the fowls of the air as a prey." The penalty at the Third Degree is "having my body severed in two, my bowels taken from thence and burned to ashes, the ashes scattered to the four winds." After that, just 30 more levels of Freemasonry to go!

Nor is there any wiggle room for Freemasons who claim they are doers of good works or 'white hats' or what have you, much less Christians. As Bible scholar David Carrico observes, in a 2018 episode of Now You See TV, even initiate Freemasons worship what they call the 'Grand Architect of the Universe'—or 'GAOTU'— "which is not the God of the Bible." The Bible is "just a piece of furniture" to Freemasonry and can be swapped out for any other religious text in initiation rites.

"Freemasonry is idolatry from the very first Degree," Carrico adds, and the GAOTU offers Freemasons a counterfeit righteousness and counterfeit salvation. Further, as co-host Jon Pounder points out, Masons ally themselves, and contract themselves by spiritual ties, to some of the worst criminals in history. In short, there is no excuse.

The cancer of Freemasonry is especially advanced in Medicine. In the book, *Medical Allusions in Freemasonry*, Bengt-Ola S. Bengtsson MD notes that Edward Jenner himself, the pioneer of vaccines, was a Freemason. So was Franz Anton Mesmer, who developed Mesmerism, and

Joseph Guillotin, for whom the guillotine is named. "Freemasons were instrumental in the development of the distinct and major branches of Western medicine that still exist today," Bengtsson writes, and "Medicine, just like Freemasonry, bridges the gap between science and religion." More recently, the Anti-Defamation League, reportedly a Freemason organization, presented its highest honour, the 'Courage Against Hate Award', to Pfizer chairman and CEO, Albert Bourla, on Nov. 10, 2022.

Of course, Freemasons and 'Illuminati' are not the only secret societies. There are Jesuits, Knights of Columbus, Knights of Malta, Knights of this, that, and the other, along with many more Satanic groups. Our nations are infested with these criminals who promote each other in public appointments and ensure corruption and incompetence are elevated alike. And once appointed, they think to issue 'mandates' on the population, when 'mandate' is the very word Freemasons use when they give orders to each other. During 'COVID', they tried to induct us into their cult without our even knowing it—yet another violation of informed consent.

Today, almost every surface institution—whether government, bank, central bank, bureaucracy, public-private partnership, nongovernmental organization, globalist club, think tank, university, army, navy, air force, police force, space force, corporation, council, or court, you name it—is the visible part of a poison tree drawing on a vast underground poisonous root. That root is the secret societies, who collude with each other to oppress, kill, and enslave their fellow man and fellow woman while covering each other's crimes with tampered evidence rooms, rigged investigations, and inverted court rulings.

Nor am I going to give the lower-level operatives a pass either, even if they are clueless about the crimes and agenda of their higher-ups, or rather, of their closer-to-Hell lower-downs. I am no more inclined to show them mercy than my merciful God who tells them, "Away from me, I never knew you!" or who called the Pharisees a brood of vipers, condemned to Hell (*Matthew* 23:33).

Secret-society members also infiltrate opposition movements to dilute their power and message or bring them into disrepute. We who have teamed up to oppose the tyrants must therefore ask each other, "Are you a member of a secret society? Have you sworn a secret oath?" Why is this question never asked on interview shows or in Congressional hearings? Of course, some will lie in response, this will only intensify their punishment when they are exposed. And they WILL be exposed.

The good news is, the Freemasons and other secret societies are going down, one way or another, and we have plenty of Old-Testament precedent for that. One of my favourites is Elijah's defeat of several hundred priests of Baal on Mount Carmel, after which he commands the people of Israel to take them down to the Kishon valley where they are slaughtered—Sudden Adult Death Syndrome by mob violence (*1 Kings* 18:40).

I used to puzzle about why the crowd acted with such brutality that day, but given the priests' penchant for child sacrifice, and the carnage I see happening again today, I am not a bit surprised now. Mob violence will return to hospitals in our time—I have seen it—with doctors and nurses lined up for retribution. Elijah also took down three monarchs—King Ahab, his queen, Jezebel, and their son, Ahaziah. Eventually, the entire house of Ahab, including Ahab's 70 sons, were put to death by Elijah's decree.

About a generation after that, Jehu ordered the priests of Baal to a ceremony in their own temple, had them surrounded by his soldiers, and each one put to the sword (*2 Kings* 10:18-27). They then demolished the temple and turned it into a toilet, an act echoing today in farmer protests that spray manure on government buildings and, I trust, on Freemason monuments and symbols along the way.

There's also the fate of Haman, the king's advisor in the *Book of Esther*, who was hanged on the gallows he had built to execute an innocent man, and this too may echo when jab pushers and skin piercers are sentenced to receive the injected poisons they inflicted on others.

Another favourite Old-Testament model for me is the close of *Isaiah 49*…

> *But this is what the Lord says:*
> *"Yes, captives will be taken from warriors,*
> *and plunder retrieved from the fierce;*
> *I will contend with those who contend with you,*
> *and your children I will save.*
> *I will make your oppressors eat their own flesh;*

they will be drunk on their own blood, as with wine.
Then all mankind will know
that I, the Lord, am your Savior,
your Redeemer, the Mighty One of Jacob."

This sounds like a secret-society ritual gone horribly wrong, a Freemason clusterfuck where, instead of drinking the blood of tortured children and cannibalizing them, they consume each other, perhaps including the punishments described in their oaths.

The ultimate Old-Testament precedent, however, encapsulating all the rest—and another example of a prophet destroying a ruler—is the annihilation of Pharaoh and his chariots in the Red Sea by the word of Moses (*Exodus* 14:28). Like Pharaoh, Freemasons have the Pyramid as their symbol, and like Pharaoh's chariots, they are racing to their own destruction.

I also draw your attention to the *Book of Enoch* which, though erroneously excluded from most Bible editions today, was written to bless "the elect and the righteous who will be living in the day of tribulation when all the wicked and godless are to be removed" (I.1). Remember I was talking just now about secret societies being a poison root? Here is what *Enoch* says (92.5)...

For I know that violence must increase on the Earth
And a great chastisement be executed on the Earth,
And all unrighteousness come to an end.
Yea, it shall be cut off from its roots
And its whole structure be destroyed.

When will all of this be fulfilled? That's not for us to know, but we sense it is coming soon. Meanwhile, I do know we are exhorted to "Resist the devil, and he will flee from you" (*James* 4:7). Let's get that done for now.

March 2024

HOW TO TRIGGER AN ATHEIST

Last weekend, I received an email from Veronica: of the family Chapman, author of *Freedom Is More Than Just a Seven-Letter Word*, whom I have quoted often in my *Battle Manuals for Freedom* series and plan to quote again. I have valued her insights into Common Law and, more recently, her heroic stand against extortion attempted by Portsmouth City Council in the form of council tax. I never even considered whether she was a woman of faith.

But, in a a flurry of emails over the weekend, from which I have her permission to quote, she denounced my use of the Bible in my latest book, *Know Your Lawful Rights*. She did try to read it, she informed me, "but I'm really sorry, Abdiel. There's far and away too much utter USELESS and IRRELEVANT God/Jesus/Biblical CRAP in it… for me. If you were to remove all of that, it could be a very good book. But it would only be about 1/4 of the size."

Usually, when I read messages or comments like this, I stop reading, press delete, and move on, but for some reason, I pressed on with this one. "But with all that in it, it's just an irrelevant and entirely useless 'distraction', that buys you NOTHING... except to distract from the real messages."

Veronica went on to tell me she's an atheist, but before I quote her any further, let me address that one statement first. It takes an awful lot of faith to be an atheist. You are trying to prove a negative. Generally, I have far more respect for agnostics who at least have the humility to admit they don't know.

And how could we know? Have you or I flown to the limits of existence, or of Space or Time, or crossed the boundaries of those limits? Have we ascended to the highest heaven or descended to the deepest abyss? Have we even explored the depths of the oceans abutting our shores?

No, so why make definitive declarations about what does *not* exist in the unseen, the unexplored, and the unmeasured? When our five senses can perceive but a tiny part of the electromagnetic spectrum, why declare what *doesn't* lie outside it?

Yet you may argue that if an atheist has no way to declare the Creator does not exist, how can a Christian declare that he does? To which I answer, I know nothing, nothing at all, and cannot hope, with the mind of a man, to encompass the unfathomable enormity of such a being. And if I ever beheld such a being, how could I live? I cannot pretend to know, only to bear witness that you and I have some inkling of what Love is and to infer it has a benevolent source, and that I can imagine no greater expression of Love than to give one's life to save another.

Also, can any atheist really be so assured of their view as to dismiss as one word, "CRAP," the treasured writings, historical accounts, poetry, and sheer literary brilliance that the Bible contains? If so, then sweep away with it Homer's *Odyssey* (which I also quote in my book), burn the writings of Plato, shred Herodotus, tear up Ovid's *Metamorphoses,* and pull down all those useless libraries while you're at it because it's all "CRAP."

Let me also remind you, Veronica and other atheists, that our enemy has deep religious motivation for the genocide unleashed upon the world in the last few years and that his murderous coordination is rooted in secret oaths and ritual blood sacrifice. What frame of reference would you have to acknowledge this if you deny yourself the context that Jesus described this religious cult as 'The Synagogue of Satan'?

And if you marvel at the pace at which tyrant technology is now advancing, would you not benefit from context in the Bible, and in the lately resurfaced *First Book of Enoch,* that tells how fallen angels, or 'Watchers', imparted hitherto hidden information to men and women who, from the outset, were thirsty to acquire harmful knowledge? Also, if there is such spiritual battle afoot as to overwhelm the senses and the perception of men, would you not value some help from he who saw Satan fall like lightning from Heaven (*Luke* 10:18)?

Also, amid the constant programming, indoctrination,

and propaganda now afoot, along with targeted stealth messaging, would you not seek protection from having the Mind of Christ (*1 Corinthians* 2:16) who called himself the way, the truth, and the life (*John* 14:6)? Unless of course, you would brand Christ a liar.

Veronica goes on, "It's really a shame that you felt it necessary to crucify yourself, but then, that does tend to be the nature of Christians, I've observed."

Now, here she gets a bit more agreement from me. Scripture does tell us that Christians have been crucified with Christ (*Galatians* 2:20), that the old has gone and the new has come, for we are new creations (*2 Corinthians* 5:17). Furthermore, it says that legal codes were crucified with Christ too (*Colossians* 2:14). Indeed, I am using this analysis in my coming book, *Know Your Financial Rights*, to point out that taxation, which relies on fictional legal codes, is dead to us, and that we are dead to taxation.

Veronica also asserts that I have squandered my free will "by continually parroting Biblical dogma, instead of using that Free Will TO ACTUALLY CREATE SOMETHING ALTERNATIVE TO THE BIBLE? You know: SOME ORIGINAL THOUGHTS?" (All the ALL-CAPS emphases are hers, by the way.) She ascribes this perceived shortfall to "a purely psychological problem, a baggage, you have brought upon yourself, at some point in your life."

Those were low blows, weren't they? Anyone even distantly familiar with my body of work will find within it a wealth of original thought, though I doubt Veronica would care to investigate, much less enquire as to what in my life's history may freight psychological baggage. More to the point, what ancient wound is now in play with Veronica so to lash out while reinforcing her own religion of Atheism?

Her diatribes also included the charge against Christians that "THEY TRY TO FORCE THEIR ABSURD BELIEFS DOWN THE THROATS OF EVERYONE ELSE." No, nothing was forced down your throat, Veronica. I did no more to incite you than write a book and offer you a free copy to express my gratitude for your contribution to the Common-Law movement.

"And CHRISTIANS HAVE TO TRY TO INTERFERE IN THE LIVES OF EVERYONE ELSE, often by throwing Biblical quotations around, like confetti." On the contrary, Veronica, it is my ardent wish to stop Government, the official religion of today, from interfering in your life or mine. As for the "confetti" comment, tell me: Is confetti refined like silver and purified seven times (*Psalms* 12:6)? Does confetti search to find just the right words, so that what it writes may be upright and true (*Ecclesiastes* 12:10)? And was confetti scattered from the hands of the Most High rather than continents and constellations?

I did not make it through all of Veronica's emails. It got to be "a bit much," as the saying goes, and I have other books to write and more fruitful battles to fight. Suffice to say she offered me the unsolicited advice "that you should remove all the God/Jesus/Biblical CRAP," and she demanded that I add to my book a disclaimer that "Veronica does not agree with the Biblical quotations, even though her work is referenced in this book." Noted. Future editions will say just that.

To conclude, this was something of a slap in the face, like the literal slap in the face the prophet Micaiah received from Chenaniah when he called out the false prophets of Ahab (*1 Kings* 22:24). Oh, but there I go again, quoting Scripture to make sense of the madness swirling around us.

I have heard occasional grumbling from readers about Bible quotations in my *Battle Manuals for Freedom* series, but nothing like the vitriol coming from vicious Veronica. Without the context of Biblical prophecy now unfolding in these times, how will she or others like her, even those in that loose assembly variously called the Truth Movement, Freedom Movement, or Common-Law Movement, ever be prepared for what's coming? When all Godless illusions are suddenly shattered, how will they ever cope with the prophetic fulfilments rushing in upon them in such an onslaught that the hearts of men shall fail for fear (*Luke* 21:26)? That is a very bad time to be an atheist and finally realize it's time to rethink your position.

Aug. 27, 2024

PART II
INSIGHTS FOR CHRISTIANS

NO, WE DON'T NEED 'UNITY'
ON THE PATH OF INDIVIDUALITY

We hear it all the time. "We need unity." After all, our enemies seem to have unity. 'COVID', for example, was a marvel of international coordination telling us the same lies at the same time, adopting the same policies, inflicting the same poisons, and passing the same tyrannical legislation (that almost everyone falsely calls 'law').

We, on the other hand, seem a motley crew of characters, shambolic, uncoordinated, and squabbling with each other over petty details. Any time some unity does appear to develop, it is either crushed by persecution or false accusation of its leaders or, more often, infiltrated by saboteurs and agents provocateurs. They pretend to represent a movement but then bring it into disrepute with bizarre behaviours and statements, or their job is simply to sow dissent and distrust among the membership. Often, the entire organization is an artificial 'astroturf' fabrication from start to finish and led by fake, planted heroes. Yes, I'm looking at you, Turning Point USA and you, Freedom Train International, among many others.

So is 'unity' truly a worthy goal for we who oppose the one-world, one-currency, one-narrative, one-religion, and one-health brigade and their puppet-masters? A few years ago, I visited Runnymede where, according to History, *Magna Carta* was first signed in 1215. This text has served as a rallying call for freedom-minded people in the eight centuries since and a model for Rights declarations. I quote it often in my books, and it is called to remembrance with renewed vigour now in this age of resurgent tyranny. I also went to the British embassy in Beijing in 2015, during the eighth-centenary celebrations, and lined up to behold the magnificent document in its glass case, and have since released those words to become flesh in us once again and to make their dwelling among us.

The most transformational impression I came away with from both of these trips was in visiting the John F. Kennedy memorial at Runnymede. To reach it, you have to walk along the Path of Individuality which winds through a wooded area to reach the stone monument where JFK's words are inscribed.

I don't remember the inscription. What I *do* remember is the plaque at the entrance, explaining that the Path comprises some 60,000 irregular blocks of stone or 'setts'. As planned, no two blocks have the same dimensions, yet they work together to fulfill the vision. They don't need to agree on some ideal set of measurements to get the job done.

Our enemies, on the other hand, are a bland uniformity. They think the same and act the same, perform the same rituals, follow the same playbooks, and sing from the same tired old hymn sheets. "You blocks, you stones, you worse than senseless things!" to quote Shakespeare (*Julius Caesar*, I.i).

Meanwhile, their followers watch television, attend mass rallies, join political parties, and conjure tears on cue. You can pay some of them to be compliant extras for crisis staging, but others will fill entire stadiums for free, and get surveilled for their troubles, to mourn the passing of manufactured martyrs and their demonic wives.

Naturally, they and their puppet-masters are threatened by our difference and independence of thought. The likes of you and me have challenged their orthodoxies, questioned their false narratives, and called out their obedience to false authority. We have been fired from our jobs, ejected from their corporations, shunned by former friends, and black-sheeped in our families of origin. Oh, and censored and demonetized and threatened.

After going through all that, are we now going to submit to another's authority, even one that is genuinely on our side, for the sake of 'unity', much less uniformity? That is not the path of the independently minded. Nor will we sign up to their blended religions that dilute the centrality of Jesus into oblivion.

Besides, the apparent unity of our foes is a mirage. Eventually, they will tear each other to pieces, as prophesied in *Isaiah* 49:25-26...

Yes, captives will be taken from warriors,
and plunder retrieved from the fierce;
I will contend with those who contend with you,
and your children I will save.
I will make your oppressors eat their own flesh;
they will be drunk on their own blood, as with wine.
Then all mankind will know
that I, the Lord, am your Savior,
your Redeemer, the Mighty One of Jacob."

I called us a motley crew. What does 'motley' mean? Definitions include heterogenous, various, diverse, and the multicoloured garb of a fool or jester. So *what* if the right hand doesn't know what the left hand is doing, or vice versa? Brothers and Sisters, fellow fools for Christ (*1 Corinthians* 4:10), welcome to this untidy alliance of motleys and misfits. You are most heartily welcome!

September 2025

REBUKING THE CROWBAR BIBLE!

"Of the increase of his government and of peace, there will be no end." That's how several Bible translations render *Isaiah* 9:7. It doesn't sit right with me, how about you? 'Govern-ment' means mind control, but the Holy Spirit is not about mind control.

When I come across something jarring in Scripture, I will search other translations to see if there's a better rendering of the Holy Spirit's intention. "To the increase of his kingdom" may be more fitting, or "of his realm."

And why shouldn't I? Translations are done by men, and men are fallible. Who knows the Mind of God but the Spirit of God? And who knows the mind of a man but the spirit of the man (*1 Corinthians* 2:11)? Then, if the Holy Spirit is joined with our spirit (*Romans* 8:16), we may discern the Mind of God. In short, we have the Mind of Christ (*1 Corinthians* 2:16).

So I have no compunction about parsing Scripture and mixing and matching translations. Similarly, I will point to Christ's irony when he tells us to gouge out our eye if it offend us or to love our enemies, and set it in the context of a corrective to misguided thought when the spiritually immature think to be justified by obedience to commandments rather than by Faith.

But do I dare to make deletions from the Bible? Here's where I call out the Bible's most glaring abomination in all of Scripture, what I call *The Tyrants Charter*. In *Romans* 13:1-7, a passage attributed to the apostle Paul, the text tells us to obey Earthly authorities and pay our taxes!

Say what now?! These notions are not only at odds with the rest of the Bible but with Paul's life and teachings, yet Mike Adams, who must now rank as the stupidest genius in all of Christendom, reacted to this passage with the headline, "Paul was a DECEIVER who perverted the teachings of Christ."

Duh! No, moron. This passage was crowbarred in by tyrants trying to corral Christians into obeying political powerbrokers. And that, as I have said, is an abomination. It is ungodly.

If Paul had an editor, he took the day off when Paul wrote this, but Paul did not write this because he could *not* have written it. A tree cannot produce different types of fruit, and this particular fruit in *The Tyrants Charter* is NOT the same fruit that we receive from Paul elsewhere. Nor, knowing Paul and his fierce temperament, would he have employed an editor.

Now, I don't have the research experience to go and find out who fucked with the Bible text, but my spirit testifies that someone did, and great is the punishment they must reap.

December 2024

DIGITAL ID — A LIVING DEATH, AND TOTAL ANNIHILATION OF SELF

Been trying to get my head around this Digital ID stuff. At one level, it seems so harmless, just let some machine take a picture of you and you're done, but I've figured a few things out about the deeper implications. Here goes...

You may already be aware that, when it comes to financial transactions, we have been assigned a fictional copy of ourselves that exists only on paper and is represented by a name in ALL-CAPS, also known as the 'STRAWMAN'. This corporate entity begins on a Birth Certificate then is duplicated on driving licences, passports, bank statements, utility bills, etc. It's not you, but they get you to believe it's you so that you will represent it and pay off the taxes, fees, fines, and debts levied against it.

It's a vile, sneaky, and Satanic system, flattening you into a two-dimensional fiction so that the parasite class can milk your lifetime productive capacity. The transactions are conducted in currencies that they print at will, then they get you to exchange your real life and labour to earn some of those two-dimensional notes (or airy digits) and then claw them back from you with myriad extraction devices such as tax forms, registrations, car parks, and speed cameras. Then they take all of that two-dimensional paper and convert it back into three-dimensional things for themselves such as cars, mansions, yachts, racehorses, and wine collections.

With me so far? Now, they come along with Digital ID. To illustrate the impact of this, go now in your mind's eye and stand outside your body and watch yourself walk up to one of those Digital ID scanners. Now hear a sucking sound and watch as your entire body suddenly vanishes into the machine.

For that is the end goal. At first, it will just be a digital copy of you in there, but then the physical you will be tied to it by a myriad of invisible strings. It's won't just be your financial life that's tied in but everything else: where or if you work, where and how you live, what you can say, do, feel, think, or even dream, what you can buy or sell, where or if you can travel, what you can eat and drink. The physical self won't be able to escape the control exercised on the digital copy, and they will effectively merge. This is the final solution. The trap is sprung, the slavery is complete.

"The 'Digital ID' they're selling you isn't innovation. It's initiation. A global ritual masquerading as convenience and security. The old rites, the sacred elixir, the connection to spirit, inverted into a code that chains flesh to machine."

— SIR ESCANOR, *FROM TEMPLE TO DATABASE: THE RITUAL OF DIGITAL CONTROL*

I have likened the Birth-Certificate fraud to a play. As soon as your beautiful, divine soul showed up, they dressed it in a costume and bundled you into a theatre, forced you to play a STRAWMAN role, and told you to memorize an alien script. But now, because electronic data is immortal, the play may live on after your body dies. Every day, the same character, wearing the same costume, playing the same part. If it is a Hamlet role, you will die the same horrible and inevitable death at play's end, only to go back to the beginning and do it all over again in perpetuity.

It is the Prometheus story for our times, he who earned Zeus' displeasure by giving forbidden technology to Man and was punished by being chained to a rock and daily having his liver devoured by an eagle. The next day, his liver is restored, only to be devoured again. It is Sisyphus eternally condemned to push that rock up the hill; it is Tantalus standing in a pool of water but never able to quench his thirst. It is an infernal immortality, it is Hell on Earth or rather, Hell in the 'Cloud'.

In short, Digital ID is the total annihilation of self, it is a living death, and *Revelation* warns us that there will come a time when men will long for death but it will elude them (9:6). Brothers and Sisters, a *real* death is infinitely preferable to the living death that Digital ID offers. Once released, the soul is set free, but I tremble to think of the implications if somehow a digital soul lives on in eternal computer simulation, and bear in mind that the eyes, and presumably iris scans, are windows to the soul.

Well, if *real* death is preferable to the future the tyrants want to impose, then so too are homelessness, exile, bankruptcy, and destitution preferable to Digital ID if that's the price we must pay for refusing. Yet we may prepare now to minimize the cost of our coming refusals. I have heard some say to keep cash going, and I agree up to a point, but who prints the cash? And who is even now printing more and more of it into worthless oblivion until it becomes more useful as fuel than financial instrument? But... they can't print silver, and they can't print gold.

They will want your consent for their digital entrapment, of course, or rather the illusion of consent for there is always coercion and threat behind it, just as there was with the infernal COVID jabs. Your consent won't make their deeds any less evil but it will help them to feel better about themselves. And they will conjure and deceive with their Freemasonic language such as 'mandate', and cook up Acts of Congress or Parliament and call it 'law', and offer 'exemption' masquerading as Mercy.

To conclude, it may seem so harmless to let a machine take a quick picture of you. Click and you're done, easy and painless, a tiny Fourth-Amendment desecration, and now go live your life as before. So it was with the quick but life-altering pricks of Pfizer, Moderna, AstraZeneca, Johnson & Johnson, Novavax, Sputnik, and Sinovac, but I hope I have helped you to see that when the camera shutter closes, so do the doors of your digital prison.

Oct. 12, 2025

THERE'S NOTHING TO FEAR IN STARMER'S DIGITAL ID THREAT

There is no terror in British prime minister Keir Starmer's threat. You've probably seen the video clip by now. He says,…

> "I am announcing this government will make a new free-of-charge digital ID mandatory for the right to work by the end of this parliament. Let me spell that out [now doing the pyramid sign with his hands]. You will not be able to work in the United Kingdom if you do not have digital ID."

"Free of charge." Oh, how generous of him. Just like the free COVID shots.

"Mandatory." This is straight out of the Freemason playbook. Ignore it. Meaningless. "Mandate" is the word Freemasons use to give orders to each other. Fuck 'em.

You're not a Freemason, and if you are, go fuck yourself, you are a child of Hell, and Jesus hates you eternally.

"The right to work." Not in any government's authority to grant or deny. Who's in charge here anyway? Who fed Starmer his delusion that thinks to tell us what we can or can not do?

If an employer wants to be in the Beast system, fuck 'em too. Be part of the brain drain that collapses their business now peopled by morons. Find an employer who doesn't want to be in the Beast system and may even pay you in gold or silver.

[pyramid sign] Yes, little Starmer wants to be acknowledged as one of the boys by his Freemason/Illuminati puppet masters and wants them to notice what a good little order follower he is. Pathetic, weak, insipid.

"… not be able to work in the United Kingdom." Boohoo. Don't work in that fictional corporate construct known as the UNITED KINGDOM, and don't pay it taxes either. Work in Britain instead, or Albion if you prefer.

Meanwhile, there's a petition to Parliament on-line against digital ID. Darlings, you can't petition psychopaths. You're supposing they are capable of empathy, but empathy died the moment they plunged their first sacrificial knife into their first sacrificed infant. And you think the illusion of parliamentary representatives safeguarding your interests is real. Oh, please!

Also, by petitioning them, you are ascribing to them a false authority and supposing that the documents they write mean anything. They don't. They're just empty contracts written by one party that negotiates with itself about how much it wants to extort, exploit, enslave, and exterminate you, then thinks to impose that contract on another party, you, without your signature or consent. Not worth the air it's written on.

Hope that helps.

October 2025

A CHRISTIAN CONTEMPLATES HIS EXECUTION (PROSE VERSION)
WHEN FACED WITH "COMPLY OR DIE"

You've likely pondered this scenario... Government enforcers come to you and offer you a choice: take this injection/ Mark of the Beast,[1] or suffer the consequences of refusal, not just poverty, homelessness, or starvation, but incarceration and death, including death by beheading.[2]

I wonder what contortions of logic they will go through to perpetrate this atrocity and justify it to themselves; what false accusations they will fabricate in service to their lord, the Accuser,[3] he who masquerades as an angel of light and whose servants masquerade as servants of righteousness;[4] what new emergency they will invent to seize emergency powers; and how, in self-righteous zeal, they may even feel virtuous in carrying it out.

But for us whom they target, the calculation begins: If I take the Mark, I get to live. If I don't, I will go through the curtain called 'Death', and I don't know what's on the other side.

And perhaps you can relate to this train of thought... Though I don't know what's on the other side, I do know that complying with the Mark would mean a living death, Hell on Earth, slavery of body and mind. The Almighty did not put me here, nor did Jesus go through his agonies, just so I could become a technocrat's slave.

Nor could I live with the pall of failure that compliance would bring, all the sorrow and regret and disappointment with myself, that's assuming I even had a sense of self left after entering the hive mind they are building for us.

I pray therefore, that if facing the ultimate test, to comply or die, I shall not comply. Though heart races, knees tremble, and mind doubts, having been assailed with lies all my life that obliteration and oblivion await me after death, I shall remember with comforts that even our Saviour wrestled and wanted out when faced with the ultimate test.[5] Yet my Redeemer lived and lives, and therefore will I live too... in him... eternally. His death was the death of Death, therefore will *my* death be *a* death of Death.

Scripture reassures us that eye has not seen, nor ear heard, nor imagination even encompassed, the wonders that are to come.[6] It even mocks Death... "Where, O Death, is thy victory? Where, O Death, is thy sting?"[7] And Love is stronger than Death.[8]

Furthermore, there will come a time when those who avoided death by complying will bitterly and even eternally regret that decision, so much so that they crave death and realize what a sweet option it was.[9] They will realize that, by avoiding a mortal's death, they entered an immortal one.

Thus, faith in the Word sustains me. Even so, I call on the mercy of the Most High—he who is gracious and compassionate, slow to anger, and abounding in love[10]—to give us further glimpses of the glory that is to come, so that when the hour arrives, the fear may be diminished.

I have already seen in mind's eye a light awaiting me on the other side of a thin purple veil, and that brings comfort, yet I still call down from Heaven to Earth more faithful visions by direct experience that see through the veil. Then may we be further reassured before we are put to the test.

Sept. 1, 2025

A CHRISTIAN CONTEMPLATES HIS EXECUTION (POEM VERSION)
WHEN FACED WITH "COMPLY OR DIE"

When they show up, demanding I comply:
Take this injection, wear this bestial Mark,
Or face the consequences; yield or die,

Will I hold fast to courage and say no
Despite all threat, inducement, accusation,
All of the trials I must undergo?

Take of this fruit, they'll say, you shall not die,[1]
Their counterfeit of immortality,
And issue 'mandates' to prop up the lie,

And maybe an 'exemption' if you say
You are a Moslem, compromise your faith,
To keep the medical murderers at bay.

Then if I take the Mark, I may draw breath,
Avoid a little longer the unknown
Of going through that curtain labelled 'Death',

Yet this is known, that saying yes to them
Would be a living death and Hell on Earth,
In thrall to demon entities and men.

I was not put here, nor did Jesus brave
The Cross, his mission, though he wanted out,[2]
For me to be a technocratic slave.

Nor could I bear the sorrow, lamentation,
The pall of failure in myself. That's if
A self survives hive-mind assimilation.

Therefore, if I should face this test, I pray,
Though heart races, knees tremble, and mind doubts,
My courage will not falter on that day.

Death means obliteration, they'll tell me,
But I'll remember my Redeemer lives,
His death the death of Death, as mine shall be.

Eye hath not seen, nor hath the mind of Man
Conceived the wonders yet to come,[3] and how
We could be chosen ere the Earth began.[4]

Scripture mocks Death: "Where is thy victory?
Where is thy sting?"[5] And Love's stronger than Death.[6]
Those who avoid death now, how bitterly

Will realize how much sweeter it had been
And long for it,[7] rather than soul entrapment,
Buried alive for all Eternity.

Faith in the Word sustains me, yet I call
To the Most High for Mercy, he who is
Compassionate and gave his life for all,

For glimpses of the Glory that's to come,
So Fear may be diminished, much as Stephen
Saw Heaven open, and the Son of Man.[8]

Behind a thin and purple veil I've seen
A light, but now call down from Heaven to Earth
More faithful visions showing Heaven's scene,

That when put to the test, we shall not fail,
Being thus comforted and reassured
To see beforehand what's beyond the veil.

Sept. 1, 2025

SNAPSHOTS OF THE END-TIMES SHITSHOW
A PORTRAIT OF TYRANNY IN QUOTES

I am rather obsessive about quotes. My books are full of them, and I have transcribed pretty much every profound, witty, or amazing thing I've ever read or heard, along with some outrageous stuff too, and built up a vast collection. As I was going through the most recent entries, I realized how powerfully they encapsulate where we are in the end-times, so here's my share. I present all without comment except for the one about the medical murder of princes.

Some are from heroes like Kevin Annett, and some from villains like Alex Karp or Peter Thiel, but I caution you not to ascribe the power of prophecy to the latter. Anything that comes out of the mouth of false prophets is, by definition, false prophecy.

Bear in mind too that the villains quoted are trying to cast spells with their pronouncements, delusionally supposing that by getting us to believe them, they will be self-fulfilling. But forecasts and projections are not prophecy, much less is wishful thinking and fantasy. (I put the notorious *Deagel Report* in that bucket too, by the way.)

One final note: I haven't assembled these quotes with my usual rigour for sourcing, as I originally intended them for personal use, so feel free to source, verify, or correct them, and to let me know.)

On tyranny.

> *Behaviors are going to have to change... You have to force behaviors, and at BlackRock we are forcing behaviors.*
>
> — LARRY FINK, CEO OF BLACKROCK

> *Our primary mission is, in fact, to set a standard for the world for behaviour.*
>
> — ALEX KARP, CEO OF PALANTIR

> *This is revolution; some people will get their heads cut off. We're expecting to see really unexpected things and to win.*
>
> — ALEX KARP, CEO OF PALANTIR

On medical tyranny.

> *Octavius was the 13th child and eighth son of King George III and Queen Charlotte. Six months after the death of his brother Prince Alfred after a smallpox inoculation, Octavius was also inoculated with the virus. He became ill, and died just a few days later [in 1783]. Queen Charlotte wrote to a friend: "in less than eight and forty hours was my son Octavius, in perfect health, sick and struck with death immediately."*
>
> — ROYAL COLLECTION TRUST WEBSITE

This whole 'vaccine' thing could and should have been stopped more than 200 years ago when 'vaccines' were killing princes. Few of us have escaped a poison needle at some point in our lives. I was force-injected by collusion between my mother and the family GP when I was seven years old. How much healthier and happier would we all be today without the sorcery of Pharmakeia.

> *The defense, through their experts, said that by being in a hospital, you are giving implied consent.*
>
> — SCOTT SCHARA, AFTER LOSING HIS COURT CASE AGAINST THE MEDICAL MURDERERS OF HIS DAUGHTER, GRACE

No court in the United States or of any State shall have subject-matter jurisdiction to review any action taken by the Secretary of Health and Human Services under this subsection.

— PREP ACT, TITLE 42-247D-6D

'Approval' is a legal fiction. All acts of FDA 'approval,' 'authorization,' and 'licenses' are legal fictions.

— KATHERINE WATT, ON THE ROLE OF THE FDA

The bio-nanoscale machines are for injecting into the body... and that is going really well with these COVID vaccines. It's going that direction. These mRNAs are nothing [other] than small scale, nano-scale machines. They are programmed, and they are injected.

— PROFESSOR IAN AKYILDIZ, PIONEER OF THE INTERNET OF BIO-NANO THINGS (IOBNT) IN A 2023 SYMPOSIUM

On legal tyranny.

A statute is a rule that government brings in, but Oliver Wendell Holmes, a Supreme-Court justice back in the 1920s, said statute without consent is not law.

— KEVIN ANNETT

Many of us are already living in a post-constitutional era, where due process is replaced by paperwork, where justice is automated and anonymised, and where citizens are processed as data... the industrialised auto-conviction industry.

— MARTIN GEDDES, ARTICLE ON SUBSTACK, JUNE 29, 2025

On financial tyranny.

Stablecoins are the bait and switch for direct-issued government CBDCs... Stablecoins can be programmed, exactly like how we fear CBDCs will be programmed. They're exactly the same tokenized mechanism... They can be taken out of your wallet. Your wallet can be blacklisted. A lot of the things that we fear about CBDCs are totally available within the tool set of Stablecoins.

— MARK GOODWIN, EDITOR OF *BITCOIN MAGAZINE*, IN INTERVIEW WITH JAMES CORBETT, JULY 2025

A federal agency can *"seize, freeze, burn, or prevent the transfer of payment stablecoins"* and specify *"accounts subject to blocking..."*

— *GENIUS ACT*, SIGNED JULY 2025

A stablecoin issuer shall have *"technical capabilities, policies, and procedures to block, freeze, and reject specific or impermissible transactions."*

— GENIUS ACT, SIGNED JULY 2025

On sexual tyranny.

You'll never develop the capacity to orgasm.

— DR. HEATHER BRUNKELL-EVANS, ON THE EFFECTS OF PUBERTY BLOCKERS

You're consigning them to a life without sexual pleasure. You're consigning them to a life where they won't become a parent. You're consigning them to be medical patients for ever.

— DR. HEATHER BRUNKELL-EVANS ON THE EFFECTS OF GENDER REASSIGNMENT IN CHILDREN

This is the direction the world is going in… We shall abolish the orgasm. There will be no loyalty except loyalty to the party. But always, there will be the intoxication of power.

— GEORGE ORWELL'S *FINAL WARNING*

On religious tyranny.

"Even the Goy who bow down to an idol, who believe in JC, deserve death penalty."

— RABBI YOSEF MIZRACHI

"What you have hunted me for is not my actions, but the thoughts of my heart. It is a long road you have opened. For first men will disclaim their hearts and presently they will have no hearts. God help the people whose Statesmen walk your road... I do none harm, I say none harm, I think none harm. And if this be not enough to keep a man alive, in good faith I long not to live..."

— ROBERT BOLT, *A MAN FOR ALL SEASONS*

On political tyranny.

Both groups, regardless what you're calling it, think that by participating in a magical ritual where they scratch an x on a piece of paper, they can give a fictitious imaginary entity they imagined into existence the right to hurt other people, to threaten them with violence, take their property, kidnap them, cage them, or kill them over completely nonsensical and victimless crimes.

— CURTIS GRIFFIN

On child sacrifice.

> The child is tortured, brutalized, terrorized. When that happens, the brain and the nervous system secrete a lot of adrenaline, and then the child is sacrificed and bled out, and that blood is collected, and it is sold. It is sometimes drunk on the spot in rituals. Other times, it is sold... They have lists, they have the name of the child, the race, the age, the quality of the blood.
>
> — MAX LOWEN, IN JUNE 2025 INTERVIEW WITH OLGA KHARITONOVA

On artificial intelligence.

> Advanced AI systems exhibit self-preserving behaviour and may soon act against us.
>
> — AI PIONEER YOSHUA BENGIO, SPEAKING ON A WORLD ECONOMIC FORUM PANEL

On transhumanism.

> Your human natural body gets transformed into an immortal body.
>
> — PETER THIEL, CEO OF PALANTIR

The new techno-religions… promise immortality here on Earth with the help of technology.

— YUVAL NOAH HARARI

On 'climate change'.

Why aren't the climate cultists up in arms about the explosion of AI and data centres, all guzzling colossal amounts of energy 24/7? Where's the outrage over that?

It seems the only 'carbon footprints' that matter are the ones left by ordinary people, not the billionaires in private jets or the technocrats building a global surveillance grid. Their consumption? Untouchable. Your heating, driving, and dinner? Public enemy number one.

Let's call it what it is: the climate change narrative is the ultimate scam, a Trojan horse for control. It's not about saving the planet. It's about enslaving you, impoverishing you, and making you feel guilty for simply existing.

While they keep getting richer, the plan is simple: Corral the masses into digital ghettos. Strip away mobility. Ban real food. And sell it all as 'sustainable.'

The worst part? It's being enabled by well-meaning people who've been brainwashed into cheerleading for their own oppression, the foot soldiers of technocratic tyranny.

And I've had enough of it.

— DOC MALIK ON SUBSTACK, MAY 26, 2025

On spiritual warfare.

He will be destroyed but not by human hand.

— DANIEL 8:25, SPEAKING ABOUT THE
'KING OF SHAMELESS COUNTENANCE'

Is God a sadist? No, he doesn't enjoy human suffering, but God wants us to grow up, and one of the ways we grow up is through suffering.

— KEVIN ANNETT

Everybody thinks there's only two choices: you're either a pessimist or an optimist. No, you need to be the realist in the middle of all that. Otherwise, you're living in a false world either way.

— G. EDWARD GRIFFIN

Then Samuel said, "Bring ye hither to me Agag the king of the Amalekites."... And Samuel said, "As thy sword hath made women childless, so shall thy mother be childless among women." And Samuel hewed Agag in pieces before the Lord in Gilgal.

— 1 SAMUEL 16:33

The illusion of freedom will continue as long as it's profitable to continue the illusion. At the point where the illusion becomes too expensive to maintain, they will just take down the scenery, they will pull back the curtains, they will move the tables and chairs out of the way and you will see the brick wall at the back of the theater.

— FRANK ZAPPA, INTERVIEW WITH JIM LADD, *ZAPPA ON AIR*, APRIL 1977

The reptilian despises the sound of bells. The moment the ringing begins, it reacts instinctively, running from the source as fast as it can. The sound is more than just a painful noise to its sensitive ears; it's a torment that cuts deep... In the presence of bells, the creature becomes powerless, unable to maintain its human disguise. The energy required to shape-shift slips away with every chime, leaving it vulnerable and exposed. The ringing not only strips away its power but also its sanity, reducing the once formidable being to a state of helplessness. The bells, harmless to others, are a devastating weapon against the reptilian, rendering it unable to function or maintain its face in the world of humans.

— SOURCE UNKNOWN

On Trump.

Trump the Chaos Mage. The Dawn of the Deceiver... Trump isn't fighting the system, he's conducting the ritual. He's the Chaos Mage of the New Aeon ushering the Age of Aquarius through spectacle, inversion, and controlled destruction. The Great Awakening you parrot like Scripture. It's not in the Bible.

It's not in ancient prophecy. It's in Luciferian doctrine where the light bearer, Prometheus Lucifer, frees man from God through gnosis and rebellion. Trump is the torch bearer. The false dawn. The new don. The trickster king… You're not waking up. You're getting initiated. The reciting the Beast's gospel to others like a missionary of inversion. A priest in drag preaching deliverance through deception. The Bible warns of a Great Deception. Not a Great Awakening.

— SIR ESCANOR (HOPIUM SLAYER) IN A TWEET, JULY 2025

On 'Jews'.

The Messiah of Judaism will be the beast of Christianity.

— ALFRED EDERSHAM

Masonry is a Jewish institution whose history, degrees, charges, passwords and explanations are Jewish from beginning to end.

— ISAAC WISE, *THE ISRAELITE OF AMERICA*, MAR. 8, 1966

Edomite Jews began to call themselves Hebrews and Israelites in 1860.

— ENCYCLOPEDIA JUDAICA

Strictly speaking, it is incorrect to call an ancient Israelite a Jew or to call a contemporary Jew an Israelite or a Hebrew.

— JEWISH ALMANAC

Fuck Israel, and if you are supporting what this rogue terrorist state is doing, you are a subhuman psychotic shit stain, and do the world a favour and fucking kill yourself.

— MAX IGAN, APRIL 2025

PART III
EXPOSING CRISIS ACTORS AND PSYCHOLOGICAL OPERATIONS

KAYLA AND THE SECRET-SERVICE CRISIS ACTORS

Meet Kayla McDonald, a red-haired, grey-eyed nurse who played a heroic role saving lives in Utah during COVID, or so we are led to believe. We meet her in an Aug. 11, 2021 public-relations video posted by Intermountain Healthcare to its Instagram account.

After the 'vaccine' came out, Kayla attests, "our unit cleared out, we went all the way down to zero." But then "the new variants came out" and numbers swelled again. "99% of our patients are unvaccinated," she laments with her hand over her heart, "and they don't need to be here, and it breaks all of the nurses' hearts."

Now meet Kayla McDonald, a red-haired, grey-eyed actress trying to make her way in Hollywood, and known for *Vulgar Fantastico* (2020), *Revenge of the Spacemen* (2014), and *The Last Lesbian* (2018).

What are the chances? In one of the clumsier crisis-actor castings of our era, the producers didn't bother changing the name of the character from that of the actress playing her.

I was content to let dust gather on my discovery of the moonlighting Kayla, but went back in my archives to find it after seeing footage from the purported assassination attempt on Trump. This seems a good time to remind you how perception is manipulated during times of emergency—whether that emergency is real or perceived or invented.

Among the clips to emerge from that day, we see a purported Secret-Service agent fumbling clumsily with her pistol as she tries to holster it. Was this just a case of professional ineptitude, or is it possible this purported Secret-Service woman was not an agent at all, not even a woke, Diversity-Equity-Inclusion (DEI) hire, but a poorly rehearsed actress, with inadequate training in stage combat, who forgot where to replace her prop?

July 16, 2024

BETRAYED BY A SANDY-HOOK CRISIS ACTOR
DAVID COLE WHEELER SOLD OUT HIS COUNTRY, SHAKESPEARE, AND ALL OF US

"For the head, aim for the head.
When they come for your rifles, give them bullets instead!"

This chorus is from a song performed by David Cole Wheeler, in partnership with actor Jamie C. Ward, for their *Ward and Wheeler* comedy show back in the '90s. They were lampooning gun-Rights advocates ready to shoot government agents who wanted to confiscate their firearms.

I was in a Shakespeare-Workout group with David and Jamie at the time. Every Saturday morning, some 20 actors would meet to play Shakespeare at Michael Howard Studios on West 25th Street in Manhattan. We would perform monologues and scenes, improvise in iambic pentameter, and share newly memorized passages from the Bard. I loved it, and the Workout sparked my enthusiasm to read every play and learn by heart the lines and speeches I treasured most.

But I remember those song lyrics too because I heard David and Jamie perform them at Caroline's Comedy Club in NYC, after which I wrote a rave review for the *Off-Off Broadway Review* in which I celebrated the comedic twinkle in David's eye. I am still connected on Facebook with a few actors from the Workout, though Wheeler himself has not accepted my recent Friend request.

I made this request after learning recently how he took his merger of art and gun-control activism to a whole new level by playing the part of a grieving father in the Sandy Hook school-shooting hoax. On the morning of Dec. 14, 2012, according to Wikipedia, a 20-year-old man named Adam Lanza shot and killed 20 children between six and seven years old, and six adult staff members, at Sandy Hook Elementary School in Newtown, Connecticut. "Earlier that day, before driving to the school, Lanza fatally shot his mother at their Newtown home. As first responders arrived at the school, Lanza killed himself with a gunshot to the head."

Among his victims, we are told, was six-year-old Benjamin Wheeler, son of David and his wife, Francine Lobis Wheeler. The next part I render in verse....

> *Then did the spotlight shine upon this actor,*
> *Brighter than he could ever have imagined*
> *If he'd remained a jobbing extra and*
> *Occasional nightclub act, winning him gigs*
> *On Oprah, Rachel Maddow, and Bill Moyers,*

Addresses to the Senate and U.N.,
And even getting flown on Air Force One!

I won't get into chapter and verse here about how and why Sandy Hook was a false-flag concoction manufactured for political ends; others have done far more extensive investigation than I; but I will examine David Cole Wheeler's role in this theatre of the absurd, or rather roles plural, because he didn't just play a bereaved parent but, later in the day of the purported shooting, posed as a paramilitary operative near the school.

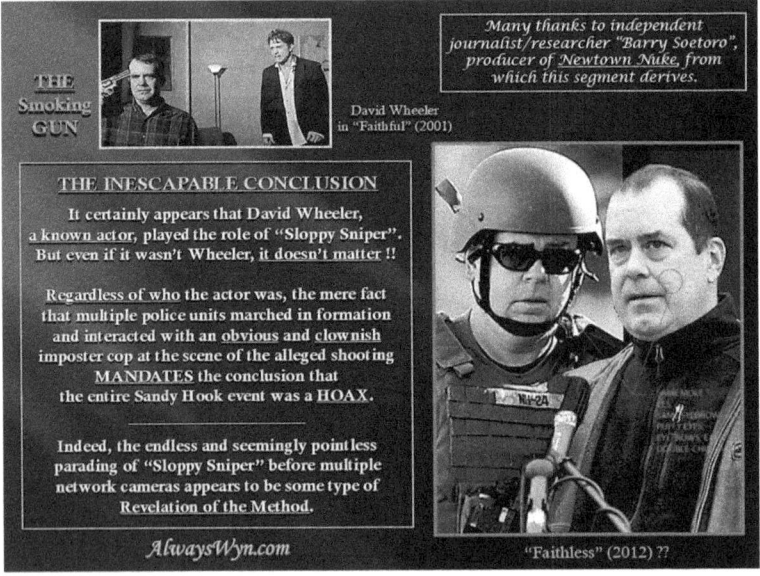

In a stunt some have labeled 'Sloppy Sniper', Wheeler appears on multiple news feeds walking back and forth in military costume that looks like it was purchased from an

Army-surplus store. Though he is wearing sunglasses, looking away whenever a camera points in his direction, and even dodging behind vehicles, he cannot hide his identity. Even the way he carries his rifle is a giveaway, holding it by the magazine in a manner that would be dangerous if the prop were real but consistent with the clumsiness of a crisis actor ill-trained in stage combat.

It was Attorney Wyn Young who brought to my awareness Wheeler's "smoking-gun" connection to Sandy Hook, whereupon I realized in amazement this was the man I had played Shakespeare with decades ago. Wyn calls the Sloppy Sniper stunt 'Revelation of the Method', but it also looks like a humiliation ritual to me.

And what of Wheeler's purported son, Benjamin? Go to the website of Ben's Lighthouse Fund, a nonprofit organization set up in honor of Ben and his Sandy Hook School classmates, and you will see photos of a boy all taken around the same age. No baby photos, no gatherings around the Christmas tree, no family photos at all except for a cringe moment with older brother,

Nathaniel, who could not look more ill at ease with the whole contrivance.

The New York Times

Francine Lobis, the daughter of Antoinette and Carmen Lobis of Bonita Springs, Fla., is to be married today to David Cole Wheeler, a son of Ann Berquist of Ordinary, Va., and Ellsworth Wheeler of Charleston, S.C. The Rev. Mary Tiebout, a Unitarian Universalist minister, will officiate at the Aldie Mansion in Doylestown, Pa.

Ms. Lobis, 34, works in New York as the personal assistant to Maureen White, the finance chairwoman of the Democratic National Committee. The bride is also a music and movement teacher for infants and toddlers in the Gymboree program in New York. She graduated from Allentown College of St. Francis de Sales in Pennsylvania.

Mr. Wheeler, 40, is an actor and musician based in New York. He performed recently with the Lexington Group, an acting troupe, at the Piccolo Spoleto Festival in Charleston and at the New York International Fringe Festival. He is also a freelance illustrator. He graduated from San Diego State University. The bridegroom's previous marriage ended in divorce.

The couple met in September 1999 at the Squeeze Lounge in New York. The bridegroom, a member of a comedy duo, Ward & Wheeler, was host to a variety show, and the bride was performing with the guest act, SwingSet, a vocal trio.

A version of this article appears in print on Oct. 7, 2001, Section 9, Page 10 of the National edition with the headline: WEDDINGS; Francine Lobis, David Wheeler. Order Reprints | Today's Paper | Subscribe

As for David's wife, Francine Lobis Wheeler, she too is an actor and singer, though her bio on the website makes no mention of her former role as assistant to Maureen White, a Democratic-Party fundraiser and member of the Council on Foreign Relations.

In recent years, I have observed the key role crisis actors play in Government-sponsored psychological operations and false-flags, and I recently exposed one of them, Kayla McDonald, who pretended to be a nurse for a 'COVID' propaganda video put out by Intermountain Healthcare. Similary, David Cole Wheeler proves to be another "poor player/ That struts and frets his hour upon the stage/ And then is heard no more. It is a tale/ Told by an idiot, full of sound and fury,/ Signifying nothing" (Shakespeare, *Macbeth*).

So this is my message to David...

I remember the comedic twinkle in your eye when we celebrated Shakespeare together, but the light has gone from your eyes now. What happened to you? Was it worth selling your soul and betraying your country for a few pieces of silver and your 15 minutes of fame? Here's what the Bard has to say to you...

> *"In the corrupted currents of this world,*
> *Offence's gilded hand may shove by justice,*
> *And oft 'tis seen the wicked prize itself*
> *Buys out the law, but 'tis not so above.*
> *There is no shuffling, there the action lies*
> *In his true nature, and we ourselves compelled...*
> *To give in evidence."*
>
> — WILLIAM SHAKESPEARE, *HAMLET*, III.III.

August 2025

TRUMP WAS STRAIGHT MAN TO BIDEN'S CLOWN

ON THE BIDEN-TRUMP COMEDY DUO MASQUERADING AS A PRESIDENTIAL DEBATE, JUNE 27, 2024

> *"Look over here, everybody. Step right up. The circus has come to town! It's the match-up you've all been waiting for: blue tyrant versus red tyrant, Democrat pussy-grabber versus Republican pussy-grabber, rock versus hard place, frying pan versus fire!"*

Everyone's talking about the Biden-Trump presidential debate as if it were real and meant something. No, they were playing a comedy duo, Trump as straight man and the actor playing Biden as clown. It was Laurel and Hardy, it was Abbott and Costello, it was Morecambe and Wise.

And it was Pinky and the Brain...

> *"Oh Don, what we gonna do tonight?"*

"Same thing we do every night, Joe. Try to take over the world."

"Oh, 'ow we gonna do that, Don?"

"Simple, Joe. We're gonna stage a comedy duo and call it a debate."

"Oh, 'Ow's that gonna help, Don?"

"It'll make the masses so distracted with the entertainment that they won't notice that we're taking away their Rights."

"Oh, that's brilliant, Don. What do you want me to do?"

"Just play dumb, Joe, act demented, like you can't string a sentence together. You can even wet your pants if you like. And I'll play the smart one."

Oh, narf!"

Remember the theme song of the show? "One is a genius. The other is insane." We watched one actor artfully play the role of feeble old mumbling, bumbling senility and the other doing his comedic deadpan response, and we had a chuckle. But the puppet master of each continued to build Hell on Earth, Biden to put up the scaffolding, Trump to finish the job, while America sat and watched, literally spellbound.

June 2024

TRUMP IS ANOTHER RICHARD III
(AND BRANDON BIGGS IS A FRAUD)

The plot of Shakespeare's *Richard III* is in play now as Trump is crowned king of a one-party state.

Richard III reigned in England from 1483-1485. He was not first in line to the throne, nor even second or third, and even his older brother Edward, who is King at the start of Shakespeare's play, took it by force. But if Richard can murder enough family members, bump off enough insiders who don't want to play along, and pull off enough theatrical feats, he may yet obtain his soul's desire.

The character's acting abilities are key to the plot. As he schemes his ambition in Shakespeare's related history play, *Henry VI Part 3*, he boasts to the audience...

Why, I can smile, and murder whiles I smile,
And cry 'Content' to that which grieves my heart,
And wet my cheeks with artificial tears,
And frame my face to all occasions.

Later, he asks his henchman, Buckingham…

Come, cousin, canst thou quake and change thy colour,
Murder thy breath in middle of a word,
And then begin again, and stop again,
As if thou wert distraught and mad with terror?

His theatrical instincts are put to the test when he pretends to be interrupted at prayer, "on his knees at meditation," as Buckingham arrives with a delegation to plead with him to become king and save the nation (*Richard III*, Act III, scene vii.).

What the delegation don't know is that Buckingham has already coached Richard in private to…

get a prayer-book in your hand,
And stand betwixt two churchmen, good my lord;
For on that ground I'll build a holy descant.

So that, when Richard emerges from his "zealous contemplation" to meet the delegation, he is flanked by two clergymen,

Two props of virtue for a Christian prince…
And, see, a book of prayer in his hand,
True ornaments to know a holy man.

Another tactic Richard uses, which he describes in his opening monologue of the play, is to plant fake prophecies and "inductions dangerous." Which brings me to that lying piece of shit pastor Brandon Biggs who, on the Ides of March this year, prophesied there would be an attempt on Trump's life, including some precise details that just came to pass.

I can't prove it, of course, but I suspect Biggs was briefed on the plan and made a public prediction that would conveniently resurface after the botched assassination attempt. Jesus warned us, remember, that there would be false prophets, wolves in sheep's clothing, and miracles to deceive even the elect if that were possible. In my opinion, Biggs is one of the supporting cast in a stage show orchestrated by another Buckingham. I venture he is following a secret oath to a secret-society brotherhood, and that is where his loyalty really lies. As Jesus—or Yeshua or Yehusha if you prefer—warned us, you cannot serve two masters, and those who pretend to do so will hear at the Judgment, "Away from me, I never knew you!"

When Trump returns to the Oval Office in 2025, I expect him to thank 'Providence' for its act of mercy in sparing his life. Then, surrounded by complicit clergymen, and to the cheers of joyous multitudes and the praises of swooning Christians, he will lead the people in prayer and thanksgiving.

Brothers and Sisters, it is all an act. Trump will do nothing to repeal the tyrant legislation—which you falsely call 'law'—that prior administrations, including his own, have cooked up. He will not break down the surveillance infrastructure nor digital concentration camps nor the *physical* concentration camps now under construction, nor will he uproot the medical-industrial complex or show one iota of contrition for the carnage his "beautiful" bioweapons unleashed. And he certainly won't break the stranglehold of that rogue state usurping the name of Israel. Yet Biggs would have us believe his man is "born again" and "on fire for Jesus" after Trump's recent brush with death. As we British say, what a load of bollocks!

There will be some token measures, of course, some hollow declarations during Trump's forthcoming honeymoon period in office. He will appear to clean house, right some wrongs, and make peace among the nations. A few token heads will roll, some guilty, some innocent, and a handful of high-profile COVID-era operatives will fall on fake theatrical swords.

But it won't amount to much. When the next convenient emergency arrives—real, perceived, or invented, most likely invented—Trump will again seize 'emergency powers'—an oxymoron, by the way, because Rights apply *more* during emergencies, not less—and crack down on the people with a level of ruthlessness and violence never witnessed before.

Trump is a serpent nestling at the nation's breast, and

his followers seem to have forgotten that he has already injected poison into the People with fangs of hypodermic steel. This most unpoetic of men has even narrated a poem that speaks of a serpent's betrayal. Once his adherents have been lulled into confidence and complacency, he will lash out against them again with vicious, bloody, and infernal bite.

One final plot point to consider: King Richard takes vulnerable children into his custody in the pretence of keeping them safe, only to destroy them cruelly behind closed doors.

July 19, 2024

THE MAGIC BULLET OF BUTLER
ON TRUMP'S MIRACULOUS RECOVERY FROM A PURPORTED ASSASSINATION ATTEMPT IN BUTLER, PENNSYLVANIA

Oh wondrous miracle, oh magical wound
To heal so fast after the bullet zoomed.
What angel watched over you as shots rang out,
What heavenly warrior in cause devout?

To see Mankind's saviour dodge a bullet or nine,
Christians are swooning, forgetting the line
That a king of fierce countenance would rise and destroy
And do it by peace and a one-world ploy.

You rallied around when your man was in court,
And gasped at his martyrdom who bravely fought.
You laughed at the farce of a thrown debate
Then anointed your king of a one-party state.

You think Trump your champion? He's Freemason made,
A Zionist tyrant, and you have been played,
And those who support him shall pay the price
If you cannot see clearer with the Mind of Christ.

August 2024

IN-AUGUR-ATION
ON TODAY'S INSTALLATION OF TRUMP

"You knew damn well I was a snake
before you took me in."
This is the line Trump loves to quote
To countenance his sin,

And still they think him their saviour
With hollering and whooping loud,
Hail him a hero and saved by God,
Those dupes in the Magatard crowd.

He staged a fake prosecution,
Anemic, designed to fail,
Then a comedy duo disguised as debate
Though you saw not through the veil,

And then that fake assassination,
How many takes to get it right?
Inflicting a wound on the upstage side,
The brighter to shine false light.

A lying pastor prophesied
This miracle to expect.
Beware, for Yeshua warned us
They'd deceive even the elect.

Trump spins his spell of dark sentences,[1]
White tile on a Freemason floor.
The Synagogue of Satan's enthroned today
And yet you cheer all the more.

He's called for torture, and didn't you hear
The Bill of Rights he assailed?
Then blasphemed the Bible in front of a church
And still your discernment fails.

He's assembled a nest of vipers
To pour poison into his ear,
Yet you think his honeyed words are sincere
To drive away your fear

Though he serves the Star of Remphan,[2]
Not David's nor True Israel's,
But tribute to Molech and pedivore diet
To sate the hunger of Hell.

You hated Biden, as well you should,
Though an actor played him throughout,
A bumbling, sniffing paedophile
Whose son was a druggy dropout,

Then hated Harris, as also you should.
You mocked, reviled, and deplored,
But this was all part of the theatre;
The opposition must fall on its sword,

So that this king of a one-party state
Could sweep in with unchallenged power
To serve a one-world government
In this his finest hour.

Davos applauds that their man is enthroned,
The globalists rejoice.
To extort, enslave, and exterminate,
He was ever the tyrants' choice.

And so America, named for the serpent,
Breathes a sigh of relief.
Behold the gilded turd now on show.
You're deluded by belief.

Jan. 20, 2025

REST IN PURGATORY, CHARLIE KIRK
ON THE SUPPOSED ASSASSINATION OF MEDIA PERSONALITY, CHARLIE KIRK

Was this the blood of Jesus washing clean
Or healing hyssop cleansing white as snow[1]
That Charlie Kirk's t-shirt remained pristine
Although he suffered an assassin's blow?

A Christian martyr dying for the fight,
Murder most foul, horrific, and obscene,
Or manufactured hero of the 'Right'
Whose stage-left exit left the fraud unseen?

This spectacle of human sacrifice,
Of pyrotechnics and special effect,
Seems a damp squib of devilish device
Conceived to deceive even the elect.[2]

'Twas theatre and devil's masquerade,
The tired old trope of a lone sniper's gun,
Another trick by which the public's played,
Conspiracy of Freemasonic scum

Whose handlers with hand signals and handshakes
Think they're superior to you and me
Just like their god, until the sulphurous lake[3]
Devours ambition for eternity.

Logic defies even a cursory glance,
The imagery that contradicts itself,
A book about it published in advance,
The propaganda flying off the shelf,

And Kirk an actor by Mossad's direction
Cannibalizing kids for Molech's lust,
Whose war is waged by way of dark deception
To fool the gullible and gain their trust.

A faction mourns, a faction celebrates,
The outrage engine cranking through the gears.
Into a frenzy, Hatred bites and bates
As media mouthpieces enflame the fear.

Trump milks the story, vows revenge, and flies
The body to its resting place, to serve
His Luciferian lord, Father of Lies,
Until the end his murderous deeds deserve.

Know Your Spiritual Rights

He promised to make great again a nation
And swore an Oath to serve the Constitution,
Yet plots surveillance and gun confiscation
While infiltrating every institution.

But Charlie, go to your appointed place
For treason to the nation's *Bill of Rights,*
Where sunlight never more shall touch your face
Deep in the kingdom of perpetual night,

To Limbo, not a place yet name it so,
"Fettered from flight, with nightmare sense of fleeing,"[4]
Nor living nor unliving, tombed below,
Your character dead, your human being unbeing.

Though you may plead to Jesus, "Did not I
Address adoring crowds to spread the word?",
He knows you worshipped the all-seeing eye
And swore a secret oath which you preferred.

Christians, if you've the mind of Christ, beware,
Be innocent as doves and wise as snakes,[5]
Sniff out the devil's schemes and be aware[6]
Lest you join Charlie in the fiery lake.

Sept. 10, 2025

THE LADY DOTH PROTEST TOO MUCH, METHINKS
ON THE HISTRIONICS OF ERIKA KIRK, WIDOW TO CHARLATAN CHARLIE

Fake blonde, fake tears, fake sympathy,
Fake hands held in her grasp
That look like they came from a waxwork museum,
And fake the entire cast.

She throws herself on the casket
Like Niobe who turned to stone.
O Frailty, thy name is Woman
Where adultery is sewn.

"I love you," she whispers, weeping in sorrow
To play her grieving part
Who so adored her crooked husband
With her crooked little heart.

Then out to the tarmac and the sound of pipers
Playing discordant dirge
As the VP's wife clutches her close
To offer consoling words.

Aye, devils will cite Scripture
Trained in Satan's finishing schools,
Groomed to be witches in holy garments,
To manipulate and fool,

Yet many fall for the hypnotic spell
And think the production true,
Disbelief suspended, and no questions asked
But for a discerning few.

It's cringy, it's tasteless, it's kitschy, ersatz,
From start to finish a lie,
Yet in the corrupted currents of this world,
As American as apple pie.

Sept. 12, 2025

JEZEBERIKA

ON THE MEMORIAL FOR CHARLIE KIRK (AT STATE FARM STADIUM IN GLENDALE, AZ, SEPT. 21, 2025), AND ERIKA KIRK'S ROLE IN IT

She comes on stage in gleaming white,
She dabs her reptilian eyes,
She soaks up a stadium's adulation and cheers
To laud Satanic lies.

Fireworks erupt to sell the image,
Molech's priestess proclaimed a saint.
To uplifting music, she whispers to the clouds
Besmeared in righteous paint.

They tell us she won a beauty contest,
A model of effortless grace,
But Trump owned the pageant, and who could resist
That little Miss Piggy face?

She forgives her husband's killer
Who not knew what he did.
Forgive him his trespass, as *she'd* be forgiven
For selling Romanian kids.

Trump's there with all his cabinet,
Musk too is on the scene.
They flash the pyramid sign to their master,
The lord of rites obscene,

And true to his Mason connection,
Trump calls Charlie Kirk 'Master Builder'.
We know what that means, and 'Tiler' too
In that club of masturbators.

Tucker Carlson comes on, likens Charlie to Christ,
Blaspheming the holy name
While a legion of lying pastors
Mythologize his fame.

A brood of vipers with lying tongues,
They peddle their vain delusion,
For the devil cites Scripture to serve his purpose
Of masquerade and illusion.

People flock to this ritual and raise their hands
And hear the Saviour proclaimed.
They praise with their lips but not with their hearts,
Yet are we not entertained?

Charlie, did you swear a bridegroom's vow
To love 'til death did you part?
Then this was the *real* bullet you dodged
To escape that Jezebel's art.

September 2025

PART IV
SHORT FICTION

THE PARABLE OF THE FROGS

There once was a group of big, fat, greedy frogs, gathered around a puddle, and in that puddle were many thousands of tadpoles, but the water in that puddle was evaporating, so the tadpoles were confined into a smaller and smaller space and feared they might die before they could become frogs.

As I said, the frogs were very greedy, and they did not want to share the land with the tadpoles, so they sucked even more water from the puddle lest the tadpoles should survive to become frogs.

Some of the tadpoles looked up and saw the wicked plan of the frogs and tried to warn their fellows, but most were too frightened to listen. A few did get the message, though, which the frogs did not like at all. "What if these tadpoles united against us?" they said to one another. "Then some would surely survive and become frogs, and who knows what chaos would ensue?"

So they decided the best course of action would be to promise survival to some of the tadpoles if they would attack the troublemakers in the puddle and silence them by whatever means necessary. The frogs also trained their recruits in how to persuade others that the real source of their woes was not the frog overlords but other tadpoles, such as those with different markings, or who preferred different ways to live.

The frogs were very pleased with themselves when they saw the conflict this caused among the tadpoles, who formed into factions and attacked each other, so that things became even more difficult in the puddle. Yet some tadpoles still looked up and saw the plan of the frogs and could not be persuaded to keep silent about it.

Then one day, those who looked up saw flying in the sky above a big white bird and, though they did not quite understand its significance yet, sensed there might be salvation in it. So they leapt from the water and splashed the surface, hoping the bird might see them. It took a few goes, but a ray of reflected light did eventually catch the eye of the bird, who looked down at the pitiful scene below.

"Well, that's odd!" the bird said to himself. "In our world, we guard our vulnerable, but these frogs appear to be doing the opposite to *their* kin."

With that, he swooped down from the clouds, and the frogs, who had been so focused on keeping the tadpoles down that they did not think to look up, had no idea of his approach until his shadow was upon them. Some tried to flee, but they were all so fat that none found the speed to get away. This way and that, the bird's murderous beak and razor-sharp talons tore into the flesh of the helpless frogs until not one was left alive!

And so, that day, the tadpoles were liberated. Fresh rains came that replenished their pool, and they could now grow freely into frogs. And as they remembered the oppression they had suffered, they did not repeat the cruelties of the first frogs, but allowed future generations of tadpoles to become themselves without fear or favour. And every year, in the season when frogs would become tadpoles, they all would sing a chorus of thanks to the great white bird who had saved them.

Of course, over time, tadpole and frog started to forget about the white bird, and it went from legend to myth to fairy tale, until most paid the story no heed at all or invented a religion around it that was really about worship of themselves. This emboldened later generations of frogs to repeat the wicked ways of their distant ancestors, who were not there to warn them of the danger.

But some vestige of the true memory remained, and whenever the frogs became wicked again, there would always be some tadpoles who would speak up and look up and call down help from the skies. And somehow, a ripple of light would catch the eye of a passing bird who would dispense his justice all over again.

Abdiel LeRoy

THE AWAKENING

Many were the souls that swept past me, their screams a vast orchestra of terror. They were flying, most of them, but there was no joy in their flight, only anguish and dread. I realized I too was mid-air, my soul also consumed with terror. And then…

That I was dead. We were all dead. Some terrible event had occurred to set us all adrift at once, dislocated spirits, suddenly removed from all we knew and loved, even our reassuring contact with the earth.

Yet, even in this state of limbo, untethered to hope, love, or connection, I began to sense that all was not lost, that we were not forever doomed to languish in agony of soul.

Some screamed still, but others, as I, began to settle and become quiet. We were waiting, and as the lamentations abated, they were replaced by a sound like rushing waters, accompanied by something like a warm breeze that brought comfort, as a golden glow began to permeate the gloom.

By now, all voices had ceased, and each of us became still, floating in air.

Then the glow brightened until it became almost too bright to behold. A flash of gold, and I found myself facing a great wingèd being so dazzling that I felt I would be consumed in his fire.

But when our eyes met, he immediately slipped into another state, his wings folded, and he became an outline in the whiteness, a moving sketch in ink, who seemed to sit before me. By now, all awareness of others was gone, and he and I sat face-to-face, as in private meeting.

But when he opened his mouth to speak, such a deafening roar came forth that once again I was put to terror. I motioned to scream myself, but no sound came forth.

Then the apparition, seeming almost as alarmed at the sound of his own voice as I, immediately put his hand to his mouth.

"Sorry about that," he said. "I'm new at this." His voice was gentle, deep, and reassuring.

Yet I was still too shocked to reply.

"Allow me to introduce myself," he continued. "I am Uriel. I stand in the presence of God."

At this, I took a deep breath as relief flooded my soul, and it was the first time since... since what shall I call it? My transmutation? My passage into another state of being?... that I even became aware that I had breath to breathe.

"I... I... I..."

"Yes, what you've experienced does tend to render mortals speechless at first, but I dare say you'll get the hang of it."

"You're Uriel?"

"Yes."

"I've heard of you. Aren't you Regent of the Sun? But you said you're new at this. So this is the first time you've..."

" 'Conveyed', we call it."

" 'Conveyed'? What does that mean?"

"Well, the battlefront's been a bit quiet of late. Not that the war in Heaven is any less intense, mind you. It's just that there's a lot more subtle stuff going on at the moment—intelligence-gathering, espionage, that sort of thing—so I thought I'd give conveyance a go. I've gone through all the training and made sure to fold my wings away when I approached you, become more human-like, and veil the fireglow. It's just my voice I forgot to change, and gave us *both* a fright. Again, please excuse."

"Um, I still don't know what 'conveyance' is."

"Ah yes, well, conveyance is when we come to souls newly released from their bodies..."

" 'Newly released from their bodies?' So I *am* dead."

"Hmm," said the angel, tilting his hand from side to side in a gesture of equivocation. "Your condition remains to be resolved, but in any case, you have nothing to fear."

"I see."

"No you don't, not really, but you will."

"So what happens now?"

"First, I need to introduce you to someone."

With that, I heard beautiful birdsong, followed by the sudden appearance of a little robin, russet of breast, tawny of tail and wings, who flew to some vaguely discernible perch between me and the angel.

Oh if I could describe his melody—so rich, so complex, so virtuous, but most of all, calming and reassuring. I had seen this little fellow often in my countryside walks in England and in its hedgerows and gardens, his presence always welcoming, always gladdening my heart. I had ever delighted in his song, but now I could discern its meaning, which I will try to set down here, however imperfectly.

"I am thy messenger, and always was,
Watched over you from Heaven and on Earth,
Prepared the way for you, from first to last,
And I was there to celebrate your birth."

Taking my lead from his manner of speech, I asked, "What is thy name?"

"You know my name," the bird replied, "for it is yours, honored and celebrated in your epic verse."

I gasped.

"I dared to hope it would be you
Who heard the prophet in a former age,
An age of wickedness, as is this one,
With new atrocity on History's page."

*"Of such atrocity I come to speak,
An intercessor now divinely sent
To counter Mankind's fear and greed and hate.
All creatures of the Earth I represent.*

*"Soon shall my kind from tree-branch disappear,
No longer shall our song herald God's call.
Birds, bees, and butterflies, from briar to brook,
Man will not stop 'til he has slaughtered all."*

I knew his message to be true, the forces of destruction to be relentless and implacable, even slowing them down a superhuman challenge, let alone stopping them or repairing the devastation left in their rapacious wake.

*"Heavy my heart to hear these dismal tidings,
That man's defilement of land, air, and sea,
Shall so persist as to extinguish hope,
Its dimming flame snuffed out eternally."*

*"But, man of God, this is not writ in stone.
If you and others like you overcome
The earthly powers now wielding their destruction,
The Will of God on Earth may yet be done."*

"But it appears that I have left this Earth,"
I countered, *"that my soul from body's split.
How then may I bring Heaven's Will to Earth
Without the vehicle to channel it?"*

Now the robin turned to Uriel, who all this while had listened in silence to our conversation. The angel interjected:

"It's up to you now. I am come to give you three choices. In an instant, I could summon a chariot of fire to take you Heaven-ward and to the eternal realms. Or, with your namesake, you could fly the skies above the Earth and gladden receptive hearts. Or, your third choice, to return to Earth as your mortal self and enact the mission just described. In any case, you will be beloved and blessed of the Eternal Father, and your choice today can neither increase nor diminish that."

Uriel now nodded to the robin who, taking his cue, flew out of our circle, piping new melodies as he left. And once more, I was alone with the angel, to whom I thought aloud:

"Better it is to be with the Lord, to follow in Elijah's wake to Heaven immediately, or to take wing with the robin, but in either case, I'd leave behind such a scene of devastation. I love this Earth and all its beauty. And though a better place awaits, I cannot abandon it now. I must go back."

"Then be it so!" said the angel.

He immediately transformed, his eyes blazing like fire, a flash of gold again, then vanished in an instant. I found myself lying on a windswept heath, staring up at a pale sky. I touched my chest to verify that I was man and flesh again, a beating heart within. Shakily, I got to my feet, and saw that others were beginning to stir around me.

They were obviously bewildered, yet I detected in

their demeanour quiet resolve. I knew instinctively that they had just experienced a revelation similar to mine. In silence, we walked toward each other until we were a small group.

"For Heaven and Earth?" I asked.

"For Heaven and Earth," all replied.

And it was so.

Abdiel LeRoy

KLAUS AND THE DEVIL

The old man wore his favourite garment for this much anticipated meeting, a long black robe with billowing sleeves and thick lapels that reflected the dim candlelight of the temple. Much blood had been spilled through the night onto the checkered tiles beneath his feet, for the cult devotees had done their job well. Since dusk, they had butchered long and hard with their sacrificial knives, while others watched, chanting and swaying in unison. And once the last drop of blood had been extracted, they practised upon each other astonishing feats of defilement.

These scenes were still playing in the mind of the man as he made his way across the alternating black and white tiles, but the temple was still again now. The floor had been hastily mopped, though the fetid odour of body fluids hung in the air. The altar itself had not been touched, and still steamed with the offal of sacrifice, dripping steadily onto the tiles beneath.

Would his shoes be stained? the man wondered. They were extremely rare and expensive, and he considered removing them before moving closer, but then he reasoned that, as they were a deep red colour to begin with, blood spatters wouldn't make much difference.

Behind the altar hung two braided curtains, fringed with gold, a slight gap between them, and a red glow pulsing from behind. The man trembled with anticipation.

"Klaus," said a drawling voice.

"Master," the man whispered back in fearful awe.

"Your work tonight was..."

"Master?"

"Satisfactory."

"Zank you, Master," said the man, though he had hoped for higher praise than this. "To bring you pleasure is our delight."

"And you did. And you did. Danke, Klaus," replied the voice.

"Bitte, Meister." He loved it when his lord addressed him in his native tongue.

"But now, we have other matters to discuss, do we not, Klaus?"

"As you wish, Master."

"Oh, be assured, I do wish. I wish very much."

"Yes, Master."

"So how's everything going with the Project, Klaus?"

"We are making good progress."

"Are you, Klaus? Are you really?"

There was something in the tone of this question that

unnerved the man. A chill passed down his body as he replied, "Yes, Master. Many have died."

"Hmm. What's your definition of 'many', Klaus?"

"Tens of millions."

"Oh dear, Klaus. 'Tens of millions,' you say. I'm afraid that won't do. There are still billions of humans running around the planet, yet you call that 'good progress.' I mean, yes you've managed to kill off some millions with the Weapon, and others have perished from famine, war, poison, and so on, but you're still woefully short of the target. Did I not instruct you to get the world's population down to 500 million? Did you not see the Georgia Guidestones before they were blown up?"

"Of course I am aware of zem, Master."

"Then you will also be aware that you are still several billion bodies short of the extermination target."

"We will do better, Master."

"Hmm."

"And ze Weapon hasn't reached its full effect yet."

"Ah yes, that brings me to another matter, Klaus, old boy. About the timing of that effect. Why did you kill off so many so quickly?"

"Master, was not extermination ze goal?"

"Yes, Klaus, extermination was *ze* goal."

Hearing this hint of mockery from his lord unnerved the man even more. For a moment, his cheek spasmed uncontrollably, until he managed to overcome his nerves.

"A for effort, Klaus," the voice continued, "but why did you kill and injure with such immediate effect? You see, with all these people keeling over just after the shot, and many of those caught on camera, you've alerted people to the danger."

"Zis was an oversight, my lord, but only because some of my colleagues were overzealous in zeir duty."

"Ha! Overzealous, you call it? Downright reckless, I'd say. You were supposed to install gradual decay into their bodies so that we might have plausible deniability, but now, with all these videos circulating of athletes and news anchors dropping like flies, people falling under trains and what have you, you have badly tipped our hand. What an appalling lack of discipline..."

"Master, I will put it right..."

"I haven't finished. Not only did you alert people to the danger prematurely, you robbed us of our pleasure in the slow torture of our Enemy's beloved creatures."

"Forgive me, Master."

"Forgive you? What do you take me for, Klaus, to suppose forgiveness is in *my* nature?"

The man had no answer, and his cheek spasmed again, and this time it took him longer to bring it back under control.

"And another question," the voice went on. "Why did you roll out the Weapon at the beginning of 2021? You made it stupidly easy for them to chart excess deaths on a year-by-year basis. Why didn't you introduce it mid-way through the year so that you could fudge the numbers better?

"We will do better with ze next pandemic."

"*Ze* next pandemic, eh? Perhaps, perhaps."

"Yes, we have ze next variant ready to go."

"Oh Klaus, now you're starting to bore me. That narrative has been going rapidly downhill since, what was it, Omicron? And then what came after, Ninja or some such? And then you got really sexy with, what, BA1 and BA2? Listen, Klaus, old fellow. How are people going to be fearful of some new variant if they can't even remember its name? Even I can't keep them all straight!"

"I understand, Master, but next we shall bring a new disease: Marburg, perhaps, or Ebola."

"They're hardly new, though, are they, Klaus?"

"But we have changed zem in ze laboratory."

"Ah! Have you now? More spike protein, perhaps? More snake venom? The problem is you have made people so distrustful after your premature kill spree that you've made it ever so much harder to mount another fear campaign. What is it those disgusting humans say? 'Fool me once…' and all of that? No, Klaus, on due reflection, I'm going to have to rethink my strategy. You and the World Economic Forum are really not fit for purpose."

A gasp of disbelief escaped from the old man's mouth, and even his best efforts could not keep his cheek spasms in check. "But, Master," he pleaded, "we did our best."

"Oh Klaus, you do amuse me. Did your best? You're starting to sound like a Christian. Our Enemy may be disposed to bestow his 'unmerited favour' on those who love him, in spite of their many failures, but surely you don't think *I'm* going to do that, do you? No, I'm going to get rid of the WEF and, for that matter, the United Nations and the World Health Organization. And I'm going to destroy them all by the hand of my real agent on Earth."

"But, my lord, am I not your agent?"

"Oh Klaus, don't be absurd. Your cover is blown, you're a laughing stock. No-one will believe you. No, the one I have appointed will appear as a saviour by going after the likes of you, but in the end will turn out to be an even worse tyrant than those he removes. Devilishly clever, don't you think, even if I do say so myself? Yes, we'll start with a soft kill at first, but it won't be long before he goes full Man-of-Lawlessness, if you get my drift. He will break you and your little Davos club, for so it is written. Nothing personal, you understand."

"But Master, all my years of service."

"Yes, I know. It's most unfortunate. All your years of service will, I fear, earn you more punishment at the hands of the Enemy. But do go on, Klaus. You're really quite entertaining."

"You promised me a reward!"

By now, the man had lost some of his fear as it gave way to deep-seated anger, resentment, and betrayal.

"Oh, that?" said the voice. "You mean you want me to extend your life? Not in my toolbox, old boy. Did you not drink enough adrenochrome then, Klaus?"

"Yes, but..."

"Did you not drink enough children? You and your chums got through quite a few tonight."

"Yes, but..."

"Ah, you mean... What was it you said in one of your boring little speeches? 'Fusion of our physical, digital, and biological identities.' Is that what you mean? You want your consciousness to be put in a chip and then keep yourself going in a machine or a skin or some such?"

"Not exactly, Master. You promised..."

"Stop right there, Klaussy Boy. I promised, did I? You do know what the Scriptures call me, don't you?"

"Yes, Master. You are called Lucifer."

"Well, yes, that's one name, but you seem to be forgetting something, Klaus, old boy."

"I don't follow, Master."

"Oh but I think you do, Klaus. Come on, you can do it. What else do they call me?"

"Ze Morning Star."

"Good. Keep going."

"Prince of ze Air, and ze Accuser."

"Bravo, Klaus, but you're still missing the key term here, old chap.

"You prowl like a lion."

"Yes, yes, yes, all of that, but you're still not hitting the mark there, Klaussy Boy, are you? Shall I spell it out for you? Shall I be plain? They call me Father of Lies, do they not?"

"Yes, Master."

"And do you suppose the Father of Lies makes promises and then keeps them? Who do you think I am? Our Enemy? Again, Klaus, you're sounding alarmingly like a Christian."

"Please, Master. Give me anozer chance. I shall bring more war, more deception, more famine, and we shall reach our target by 2030. We shall have more bioweapons, energy weapons, poison ze water, ze air, ze food, more radiation, more censorship, more surveillance, more legislation, cyber attacks, quarantine camps, more taxes and fines and fees to break ze will of ze people, und so on."

"Oh, Klaus, aren't you adorable? Bargaining with me to procure what? Mercy? I don't do mercy, Klaus. You should know that by now. 'The quality of mercy is not strained. It droppeth as the gentle rain from Heaven upon the place beneath.' Blah Blah Blah. Das ist Qwatsch, Klaus!"

The man's knees were shaking now, whether from fear or anger, an effect heightened by his interrogator's return to his native language, not to praise this time but in rebuke.

"Of course, I'm not into rain, either," the voice continued, "not normal rain, I mean. I go in more for tornadoes, hurricanes, earthquakes, floods, forest fires, you know the type of thing, what they foolishly call 'natural' disasters."

"Please, Master, I beg you..."

"Ah, that's more like it, Klaus, begging me, acknowledging my power over you, but it's still too late, old boy. You see, I've grown weary of you. Now run along and tell Justin to come in. He's waiting outside. I'm in need of some stimulation of a more physical nature, and he always proves most willing to oblige."

"Master, I could perform zis function if you wish."

"Oh, Klaus. The very thought. How revolting. Do I seem that desperate to you?"

"Zat's not what I mean. I mean I can do... ze special zings."

"Oh where have I heard that before? Let me think. Emmanuel said it, Rishi said it, Tony said it, Boris said it, Jacinda said it, and so did Chrystia, Ursula, and even horrid little Theresa. And yet every single one of them profoundly disappointing, I do assure you. Quite without personality, wholly without charm. And, come to think of it, since they're all your little acolytes, Klaus, I really thought you would have trained them better.

"Now, don't get me wrong. It's not that I'm especially fond of Justin. The boy is an absolute dullard, and even dimmer of intellect than all the rest of you, but he is at least accommodating, and that shall suffice for now. Come to think of it, Klaus, do you know who else was in here just the other day offering me 'special zings,' as you put it?"

"I don't know," the man replied wearily.

"Your mate, Charlie boy Windsor! Well, of course, I was so disgusted by the very *idea* of old Sausage Fingers coming anywhere near me that I was tempted to put him out of his misery right there and then. But alas, I'm not permitted to until the Enemy tells me it's time, and apparently, his crimes must be revealed first. Which won't be long now, of course. The Kamloops and Caernarvon revelations are well underway."

"Master, I could bring more evidence against him."

"Down to your last straw now, are you, Klaus? Throwing your friends under the bus to buy yourself a little more time? No, Klaus, there's no need. His fate is sealed... as is yours. Now then, entertaining as this discourse has been, I have other matters to attend to. I'm sure you can understand the burdens of running a global empire. Permit me to dispense with the customary pleasantries such as 'Goodbye' or 'Farewell', much less 'God bless you'. In your case, none of them applies."

"Master! Master!" the man called desperately, but it was all in vain. The red light behind the curtain dimmed to an almost imperceptible glow, and Klaus knew in an instant that all his life's work was for naught. Soon, he would join his mentor Henry in permanent exile from life.

Perhaps that had been the plan all along, to use him and then to discard him as so much medical waste. He would be dead within the day, he was sure of that.

Barely able to stay on his feet, the man shuffled his way back across the checkered tiles and out into the hallway. There, sitting anxiously on a chair beside the wall, was little Justin, ever eager to please. He rose to greet his tutor and extended his hand.

"Hello Klaus," he said with his ingratiating smile. "Good to see you again."

Klaus did not return the gesture, didn't even turn his head to look at the supplicant awaiting his turn to enter the chamber. "Fuck off, you little shit!" he replied, and marched resolutely towards the front door.

Two security men followed him to the vestibule, but Klaus dismissed them with an impatient flick of his hand. Not even an army could protect him now. He put on his coat, eager to cover the expensive robe which now seemed so preposterous, even to his own eyes.

Off came the red shoes too. He didn't even bother undoing the laces this time but held down the back of each shoe with the front of his other foot and hurriedly peeled them off. Cursing under his breath, he picked up his normal shoes from a shoe rack before him and slipped them on. His hands were trembling too much to tie the laces so he left them loose.

He made his way out of the front door and staggered down the front steps of the lodge. The air was cold, and a dim light ahead signalled the beginning of a new day, the close of which he did not expect to see. He took a few deep breaths of the chilly morning air and felt a giddy delight as condensation formed from his breath. These may be his final moments, but at least he would enjoy this last palpable token of life.

His path led him past a garbage bin, where he tossed the red shoes, then towards an old church on his right. It had a sad, dilapidated look to it now. There had been many more funerals there of late, but fewer weddings, and hardly any christenings. Its life was hanging by a thread. He had achieved that much at least, the man thought to himself. Should he go in there now and confess his sins? He laughed at the idea. "Too late for zat now, Klaussy Boy," he chuckled to himself, recalling snippets of the chilling conversation he had just had in the temple lodge.

On the next block, he walked past a school playground where, soon enough, the din of playful children would be heard. "We didn't kill enough of you," he whispered to himself.

Immediately, his mind began weaving the old equations, how a rising death count would promote him in the eyes of his collaborators in the secret society, and how the youngest victims would count the most because they were closest to the God he hated. The ones who survived would be trained and traumatized to become wholly indifferent to the suffering of others, a generation of cold-blooded killers, ready to follow orders without question and complete the work of annihilation.

Klaus stopped, placing his hands on the chain-link fence outside the playground, looked in, and sighed. At that moment, a ray of sunlight kissed the side of his face.

"You know this will be the last time you feel the sun, don't you?" said a voice on his left.

Klaus turned to see who had spoken. A man was standing beside him, wearing a white robe that shimmered in the morning breeze. He too was looking into the playground, but his eyes shone as white fire.

It was time.

Abdiel LeRoy

FROM THE AUTHOR

Thank you for reading this book, the final installment of *Battle Manuals for Freedom*. If you have found it helpful, I would value your review wherever you buy books. A few sentences would suffice.

If you think I've missed something important, or a link doesn't work, or you find some other glitch, send me an email to RenewedTestament@protonmail.com. I am quick to make adjustments when readers point out errors or omissions.

If you'd like updates from me, join my mailing list from my website, PoetProphet.com. I also post articles to Substack at *The Poet's Eye* (though I have been 'demonetized' there) and occasional videos to the 'alternative' video-hosting sites, BitChute and Brighteon.

I don't bother with TikTok any more after it closed one of my accounts and savaged my remaining content with strikes and shadow-bans, and I gave up on Facebook, YouTube, and Twitter long ago.

One way to support my work is to join the United Precious Metals Association—at Geni.us/UPMA—and send over a goldback or two, easily accomplished via my email address. But the best way is to buy and review my books. My titles encompass fiction, non-fiction, memoir, poetry, and epic poetry, all listed below. You can avoid Amazon entirely now by buying direct at https://payhip.com/poetprophet.

When it comes to this series, I recommend the paperbacks if you're using them as battle manuals, then you can mark them up with notes, labels, and highlights for quick reference, but if you want to dig deeper, the eBooks will serve because they contain links to my on-line sources.

I don't offer individualized advice services, however. Sometimes, I hear from a reader, or someone who has watched one of my videos, setting out a lengthy description of their circumstances and asking what actions I suggest. I want to help, but my immediate calling is to write books, and I hope that shall suffice both to benefit you and to reward me. I also echo Tolkien's observation that "advice is a dangerous gift, even from the wise to the wise."

Finally, thank you for embracing this labour of love. May the Most High bless you and keep you, make his face to shine upon you, and give you everlasting life. May he go with you and ahead of you, a pillar of cloud by day and a pillar of fire by night, and bring you to places he hath prepared.

Abdiel LeRoy, 2025

BATTLE MANUALS FOR FREEDOM
GENI.US/RIGHTS

Book 1: *Know Your Medical Rights*
Book 2: *Know Your Lawful Rights*
Book 3: *Know Your Financial Rights*
Book 4: *Know Your Spiritual Rights*

BOOKS BY A. LEROY
(ABDIEL LEROY)

NON-FICTION

KNOW YOUR MEDICAL RIGHTS

Did you know that, under international law, no-one can demand you get a medical test, wear a mask, or have any other medical procedure?

And did you also know that no emergency, even if it threatens the life of a nation, takes away any of your rights? Or that any politician or pundit who attempts to persecute a group based on medical status is committing a Crime Against Humanity?!

Meanwhile, international law also confirms YOUR MEDICAL STATUS IS CONFIDENTIAL, a protection supported by medical codes dating back millennia to the Hippocratic Oath.

Yet governments are not only demanding we hand over this sacred information but are still using it to divide and discriminate, penalizing bodily sovereignty and autonomy, and they are poised to inflict even worse atrocities than they did during 'COVID'.

"I know in my heart that these measures are an atrocity," writes Abdiel LeRoy in the Introduction, "and my spirit rebels against them, but just having that instinct is not enough now. WHAT ARE MY RIGHTS?"

Here is your constitutional Bible, a rebuking voice to tyranny, and a rallying cry for all Mankind.

KNOW YOUR LAWFUL RIGHTS

Not since the days of Noah has Earth witnessed such an all-out assault on life and livelihood as we see today. The false authorities are pursuing their agenda of extermination and enslavement with a ruthlessness most of us could never have imagined.

In this sequel to *Know Your Medical Rights*, Abdiel LeRoy dismantles the lies, programming, and conditioning that have kept us from ourselves. He reminds you who you are, a three-dimensional being standing above the two-dimensional fictions of government, and he empowers you to tear down strongholds of dogma and dictatorship.

"I will show you that all is counterfeit, all theatre," LeRoy writes in the Introduction, "and that counterfeit governments, issuing counterfeit currencies and writing counterfeit legislation masquerading as Law, are wielding counterfeit authority. It's so much easier to refuse and refute that authority when you know its enforcers are beneath you and that they are peddling fictional constructs."

Then, having pierced through the illusions and mind-tricks of tyrants, he lays before you the weapons of True Law you will need to regain your Sovereignty and Birthright. This book will serve you as armour and weapon in the battles ahead.

KNOW YOUR FINANCIAL RIGHTS

Your tax compliance has been funding genocide. Your debt payments are rewarding banks who never lent you anything in the first place. Meanwhile, any digits in your bank account can be seized or freezed at a moment's notice.

The entire financial system has been engineered to extort us, enslave us, and then finally to exterminate us when we've nothing left to give. It's time to tear it down and stop funding our demise, and it's time to transact in ways that tyrants can not monitor, surveil, and control.

Know Your Financial Rights is the final installment of a tyrant-slaying trilogy of constitutional bibles, recalling the mission of Bible prophets who overthrew kings.

Wear this book as a garment of protection, wield it as a spiritual sword, and weaponize it against those who are now conspiring against us.

KNOW YOUR SPIRITUAL RIGHTS

You know it's coming, spiritual battle on a scale never seen before. Are you prepared? Will you take hold of your authority to overcome all the power of the enemy? Are you anchored in the Mind of Christ so that no deception can sway you? Are you fortified in your faith?

This vook will serve as sword and shield in the End-Times ahead.

Know Your Spiritual Rights is a full-on, no-holds-barred, in-your-face weapon to tear down Satanic strongholds and to inflict catastrophic spiritual violence against enemies of the Most High. If you have no stomach of the fight, then this book isn't for you.

THE GOURMET GOSPEL COLLECTION
A Better Eden/ It Was for Freedom/ Foes to Grace

Desperate to escape from an eating disorder, Abdiel went on a quest for "the truth that sets me free," and found it in a rediscovery of Grace—the unmerited favor of God—that church teachings rarely, if ever, reveal.

With the help of great writers, Christian thinkers, and of course the Bible itself, he returns to an Eden of the mind that predates the command, 'Do not...', and where sin is neither possible nor perceived.

DUELING THE DRAGON COLLECTION
Five Memoirs About Living and Working in China

A wide-eyed expat is detained by Beijing cops and told to sign a false confession. Will he make it out of China alive? *Dueling the Dragon* is a great adventure story, but *this* one just happens to be true!

With a journalist's eye and lively wit, LeRoy's memoirs expose the deep levels of corruption tearing at China's social fabric.

MY PORTABLE PARADISE
Transform Your Life Through House Sitting

Tired of burning bitter hours in a toxic job? Tired of the same old routine? Tired of the stress and hassle of paying rent, or a mortgage? Then house sitting may be for you.

From a beach house in Costa Rica, this veteran house sitter and author welcomes you to share in the joys and blessings he has received.

Whether you're a 'digital nomad' looking for adventure, retired and seeking a change of scenery, or just looking for a simpler life, you'll find gentle guidance in this book. And... it might just change your life!

POETRY COLLECTIONS

WELL VERSED
To Shakespeare, Poets, and the Performing Arts

Dante is famous. He imagined Hell,
A plain of burning flakes and sulphurous smell,
Pour souls afflicted in a sorry state,
And names the enemies he loves to hate.

But he's no match for Milton's inspiration,
No poet greater in imagination.
Yet Shakespeare most gets ink within these pages.
'Twas he who said, "Our praises are our wages!"

VERSES VERSUS EMPIRE
I—The Bush Era

It's Judgment Day, and George W. Bush strides confidently towards the throne of God. How will the Almighty respond? Find out in this work of devastating satire.

From Bush through Obama to Trump, LeRoy charts an epic course through the inferno of U.S. politics, exposing the fraud and folly of empire and its rulers.

VERSES VERSUS EMPIRE
II—The Obama Era

As the late historian Howard Zinn said, "There have only been a handful of people who use their wit to take down the pretensions of the high and mighty."

Here is one of them, a resounding voice for our times, an offering of hope and beauty rising from the ashes of a broken political system, a creation of unprecedented literary power. Witness herein that the pen really *is* mightier than the sword!

VERSES VERSUS EMPIRE
III—The Trump Era

The intellectuals of this dangerous age,
However eloquent, however sage,
Indicting empire with insightful prose,
Have not yet healed the nation's woes.

To tear down strongholds of the powers-that-be
Who give lip service to Democracy,
A poet of prophetic voice steps forward
To prove the pen is mightier than the sword!

VERSES VERSUS EMPIRE
IV—The Biden Era

A mumbling, bumbling, fumbling, stumbling actor
Playing Joe Biden takes the stage to build
Satanic tyranny and hell on Earth,
Totalitarian prophecy fulfilled,

But Scripture tells how, by their words alone,
Prophets killed politicians, kings, and priests,
And many of those words written in verse,
For poetry defeats the End-Times Beast.

THE VERSES VERSUS EMPIRE COLLECTION
Poetry and Prose on Four Imperial Presidencies
2001-2025

Through four imperial presidencies
The poet cries, voice in the wilderness,
Reed swaying in the wind,[1] a bruisèd reed,[2]
His motion stirred to music,
Daring to see and state the obvious,
Decry hypocrisy, prophetically to see
Not just the future but the now,
The awful now and make some sense of it,
The world a stage on which plays out
Congressional pantomime, a knot
Unable to untie itself. The blood
Of innocents cries out to Heaven where
These incensed lines as incense burn
With hate of Hate and hope of Hope.

EPIC POETRY
(FICTION IN VERSE)

ELIJAH
The Great Prophet's Life Retold in a 12-Chapter Epic Poem

He called down fire and false prophets slew,
He raised the dead, conversed with angels, flew
To Heaven in a chariot of fire
And fled from Jezebel's murderous ire.

But there is more, O so much more to tell,
Of meeting Moses and a dragon's spell,
Shapeshifting goddesses at Cherith Brook.
Such wonders will unfold within this book!

OBAMA'S DREAM
The Journey That Changed the World

This sordid theatre we call politics
Is full of lies and dirty tricks,
But what if angels came into the fray
To challenge presidents and what they say?

And what if one appeared before God's throne
Where wicked schemes of men are overthrown
And Satan tried a victim to condemn?
This book turns upside-down the world of men!

THE EPICS COLLECTION
Obama's Dream, Elijah, Jezebel's Lament

It is an age-old struggle, that between
The earthly power of presidents and kings
Encountering divine power, wonders seen
When prophets pray. This theme the author brings

In reinvention of the Bible tales,
Ascents to Heaven, wondrous revelation,
Shapeshifting goddesses in his portrayals,
Joined by the author's audiobook narrations.

FICTION

JEZEBEL'S LAMENT
A Defense of Reputation, a Denouncement of the prophets Elijah and Elisha

In this companion piece to *Elijah*, Israel's tyrant queen tells her side of the story and why she so detests that "unkempt fire-and-brimstone hairy hermit" who prophesies dogs shall eat her corpse.

"Yes, I had to get rid of some inconvenient men of God along the way, and a stubborn wine producer, but in all this I did only what a queen *must* do in such circumstances to protect herself, to safeguard her family and the royal line."

You will hear of trysts and treason in this witty rendering by Abdiel LeRoy.

THE CHRISTMAS TREE
A Tale of Divine Awakening

A tree is torn from his forest home and all that he loves, but there is courage in the heart of a little boy to protect his belovèd tree.

The author dreamt up this story from witnessing Christmas trees being abandoned on city sidewalks, but here his invention of a magical journey for one such tree will transport you through time and space and otherworldly encounter, even to the throne of God!

THE PRINCE'S OATH
A Tale From Afghanistan

An innocent man must lose his freedom, an innocent girl must yield her virginity, in this traditional tale from an era of kings.

From bandit attacks in a forest to treacherous plots at court, love will undergo many trials with the Almighty's help, even if it comes in the form of a cheeky little mouse!

THE CHRISTIAN REVERIES COLLECTION
The Christmas Tree/ The Prince's Oath/ Obama's Dream

You'll know a tree according to its fruit,
Three golden branches with one holy root,
The Good Book's inspiration running through,
This trinity uplifting hearts anew.

Not 'R'-rated as the Epics Collection,
These tales are more of a 'PG' selection,
But still have magic, shapeshifters, and all
Those elements mythology recalls.

NOTES

"It's the Jews!"?

1. Judah continues, saying Bathshua's father "showed me a boundless store of gold in his daughter's behalf; for he was a king. And he adorned her with gold and pearls, and caused her to pour out wine for us at the feast with the beauty of women. And the wine turned aside my eyes, and pleasure blinded my heart. And I became enamoured of her, and I lay with her, and transgressed the commandment of the Lord and the commandment of my fathers, and I took her to wife... for the sake of money and beauty I was led astray to Bathshua the Canaanite."
2. From Pharez came the royal house of David; from Zarah, I am told, came the kingdom of Troy, with Priam, Hector, and Aeneas.
3. I treasure these words. My first professional acting role was playing Jesus in a series of passion plays, and I auditioned with this speech, having reworked it into iambic pentameter.

Traitor Trump

1. https://www.youtube.com/watch?v=IHKEfDs3qYU
   https://old.bitchute.com/video/AKYd9CMex6s2

A Christian Contemplates His Execution (Prose Version)

1. *Revelation* 13:15-17.
2. *Revelation* 20:4.
3. *Revelation* 12:10.
4. *2 Corinthians* 11:13-15.
5. *Luke* 22:41-44.
6. *1 Corinthians* 2:9.
7. *1 Corinthians* 15:54-55.
8. *Song of Solomon* 8:6-7.

9. *Revelation* 9:6.
10. *Psalms* 103:8, 145:8.

A Christian Contemplates His Execution (Poem Version)

1. *Genesis* 3:4.
2. *Luke* 22:41-44.
3. *1 Corinthians* 2:9.
4. *Ephesians* 1:4.
5. *1 Corinthians* 15:54-55.
6. *Song of Solomon* 8:6-7.
7. *Revelation* 9:6.
8. *Acts* 7:56.

In-augur-ation

1. *Daniel* 8:23-25.
2. *Acts* 7:43.

Rest in Purgatory, Charlie Kirk

1. *Psalm* 51:7.
2. *Matthew* 24:24.
3. *Revelation* 20:10.
4. A line from the poem *Limbo* by Samuel Taylor Coleridge.
5. *Matthew* 10:16.
6. *2 Corinthians* 2:11.

Poetry Collections

1. *Matthew* 11:7.
2. *Matthew* 12:20.

www.ingramcontent.com/pod-product-compliance
Lightning Source LLC
LaVergne TN
LVHW051216070526
838200LV00063B/4915